FOUR SEASONS

TWO CONTINENTS

A collection of short-stories, prose and poems by members
of Oswaldtwistle Writers, Lancashire, England and
Rowville Aspiring Writers, Melbourne, Australia.

Photograph from
Stock

Cover Design by
Nicola Ormerod

Dedications:

Rowville Aspiring Writers

Proof readers: Margaret Gregory, Heather Hodge, Arthur Ives, Beverley Prosser and Barbara Scott.

Co-ordinator: Arthur Ives

Oswaldtwistle Writers

Proof readers: Charlotte Youds, Arthur Ives, Linda Wahlers, Peter Jones, Peter Moulding.

Sub-editor: Charlotte Youds

Editor: Peter Jones

Rowville Aspiring Writers

Our Rationale

To share our work and to enjoy the work of fellow writers.
To receive criticism with good grace.
To consider suggested improvements.
To gather knowledge to raise the standard of our writing.
To provide an audience
for the appreciation of our efforts.
And, by meeting together, to be stimulated to work towards
and achieve, the goals we each have set ourselves.

About Us

We are a mixed group with very different creative styles and skills. For our main meeting, we gather on the fourth Tuesday of each month from 1pm until about 3pm at the Rowville Library, under the clock tower at Stud Park Shopping Centre, Rowville, Victoria. We also have a workshop on the first Tuesday of the month at the same location and times, to examine different aspects of the writing art.
Newcomers or visitors with interests in writing are always welcome.

Oswaldtwistle Writers

Oswaldtwistle Writers were formed in 2010, when Peter Jones, already a library volunteer approached library manager, Susan Jabbari about the possibility of starting a writers' group within the library.

The group meets on the second and fourth Monday of the month at Oswaldtwistle library, Lancashire, England and have been flourishing ever since. We run occasional workshops and set voluntary projects at each meeting. Our goal is to be accessible to writers of every genre and ability.

Our association with Rowville Aspiring Writers came about through the daughter of one of our members being a part of that group and we have a very healthy respect for them as fellow writers and relish the diversity that comes from a meeting of two countries, culturally and geographically.

Contents

SPRING

The Cuckoo...2

Spring Drizzle..3

Spring...4

The Hawthorn 5

The Spring Launch 7

A Season for every Purpose.............................9

Bearly Spring...17

The Rites of Spring...21

Spring...22

Spring Song 23

Objects In The Rear View Mirror...................24

Four Seasons? Totally confusing....................25

Spring Rains...27

Spring Forward 29

Spring into Action! 30

Spring is Here 32

The Four Seasons..34

SUMMER

Summer..37

June, Lake Cascade, Idaho..............................38

A Period of Refreshment 42

Sweet Surrender..46

Summer of '70 Point Duty..............................47

Crosby Sands 63

A Summer's Day 64

Four Seasons......................................66

Scents of Summer 76

Summer Sonnet....................................79

Trevor and Tippy's Summer Holiday.............80

Summer Splendour 83

Sound Bites......................................86

Uncle Utu's Seasonal Umbrella....................87

Summer Story 91

My Apple Tree.....................................95

AUTUMN

The Nose Knows...................................97

Passages of Time 99

Chronicles of young Love 104

Autumn Evening...................................117

Autumn in New England 118

An Autumn Tale 119

Autumn Morning 125

Changing Seasons.................................127

Autumn 128

Mold...129

Fall 130

Reflections of change 131

WINTER

Dining Out 133

Rowan Trees 134

Creation's Secrets 137

A Long Day for Eva 139

A Winters Tale...143

Christmas is Cancelled 148

Mags and Maggie 152

My Winters Remembered............................155

Winter Soul...157

Otto's Winter Heist 161

Sometimes...164

Seasoned Greetings from Oz 166

Winter, What Winter. 168

Winter 173

Snowflakes..174

The Peaceful Garden....................................175

Winter 179

The Summer Storm at Christmas.................180

Winter's on the Way....................................183

Zodiac. 185

Spring

Four Seasons

The Cuckoo

Eric Braysford

Check out that sound in the distance!
Echoing so soft, yet so clear;
CUCKOO! CUCKOO! The harbinger's voice,
Announcing that springtime is here.

Those proud, melodic, dulcet tones,
Proclaiming its name from afar;
Belie a bird like no other,
With behaviour strange and bizarre.

Cursed as a villain of nature,
For no territory will it defend,
No elaborate courtship to witness,
And no nest-building time does it spend.

Watching, waiting, ready to pounce!
Some unwitting suspect to cheat,
She lays down an egg to be fostered,
Her maternal instinct complete.

And when the dastardly deed is done,
The cuckoo shall fast disappear,
Flying due south to warmer climes,
'til springtime approaches next year.

Spring Drizzle

Carol Cooper

Three frogs leave the water,
Bent on juicy frogs to slaughter,
(They enjoy the mist and damp).
Drizzly evenings, light fails early,
Yellow lamps in windows blurry,
Show cats indoors warm and purry.
Now fledglings take their evening bath,
Unafraid of feline wrath.
Despite the wet clothes on the line.
I'm glad it didn't turn out fine.

Spring

Wendy Sanderson

Spring is like the birth of a child. It has slept in the dark for months, waiting for that subtle change in its host. Its passage slow and laboured, as it makes its way from total darkness and seeks out the faint light. It slithers its way, gently, gently, pushing tiny tendrils and unfurling leaves reaching for the sunlight which will aid their birth. Then nature sometimes seems to pause; as with childbirth, seems to pant and keep things on hold. Then suddenly, as if it can wait no longer to live life, it bursts forth, prompting the oohs and aahs at a new untainted life, so full of innocence. To be loved, cherished, bringing so much happiness. And as it grows and is nurtured, we experience the birth of spring, yet again.

The Hawthorn

Eric Braysford

The Hawthorn is a common sight,
by woodland, hedges, and brook.
The ragamuffin of all trees,
not worth a second look.
Its twisted limbs, with jagged leaves
and shape all seem to say,
"Don't come near me, I know I'm ugly,
Clear off! Keep away"!

For something happened long ago,
that bows its head in shame.
Some great event in history;
A story of legend and fame.
Perhaps the Hawthorn's finest hour,
or a lifetime's curse instead.
That moment when its crown of thorns
was placed upon Christ's head.

But God is so forgiving
in His own redeeming way,
and takes the Hawthorn to His heart
in the merry month of May
He showers those limbs with blossom
like an icy waterfall;
A pure white image of Himself.
The noblest One of all.

Four Seasons

So If you're out for a ramble
or an afternoon stroll before tea,
just pause and take that second look
at the humble Hawthorn tree.

The Spring Launch

Mary J O'Rourke

"Bit nippy this morning Fred. Where are you off to at this unearthly hour"? enquired Kate.

"Just to collect my Sunday paper, it hasn't been delivered again. And where might you be off to, lassie?" He always called her lassie.

"Oh, it's the Spring Launch tomorrow and there's lots to do you know, so me and the girls will be there all day."

Kate slowed down to keep pace with Fred. "You'll have to call into the shop tomorrow. It's free coffee and biscuits and you may just see something you fancy." Kate wished Fred a cheery "Good-bye" at the paper shop.

It was a cold, clear and frosty early March morning and it looked like the day promised to be nice later on. Kate arrived at the 'ladies and gentleman's' shop in the deserted market square just ahead of Barbara and Alison, her two trusty and hardworking assistants for the day.

"Morning girls, let's get the kettle on for a cup of tea. First things first, then we'll get started," said Kate cheerfully.

Before they knew where they were, it was almost 12 noon and lunchtime. They had turned the shop inside out, upside down and back to front. What had been left of the old winter stock and sale items had been listed and packed away ready for collection in the morning by the delivery driver who would be dropping off a further back up consignment of new Spring and Summer stock. The

7

Spring Launch was due to start at 11am the next morning, so there was still lots to do.

After a leisurely and chatty lunch the girls were soon back at work. New stock was put in situ, mirrors polished, pictures rearranged, vases of silk spring flowers appeared as if by magic. The window dummies were next, they needed to be dressed, three for the men's window and four for the ladies section.

Donald, Hughie and Gordon, as the boys were affectionately known, were soon dressed and looking rather smart in summer shirts and slacks. The Beverley Sisters always looked pretty and demure in their colourful skirts and blouses. Jezebel wore shorts and a T-shirt.

The backdrop was completed and the base of the huge window was covered in artificial grass with daisies dotted here and there, a couple of cane chairs and a table with glasses of lemonade. Some balloons and streamers completed the picture.

The girls stepped out onto the pavement to admire their handiwork, and all agreed that they had made a good job of it.

"Right, let's have another cup of tea, a quick tidy around and that's it," said Kate and she lowered the blinds, so that no one could see their window until tomorrow at the Spring Launch.

A Season for every Purpose

Margaret Gregory

The tall red headed man, dressed in a brown full-length cape, stood in the open plaza. The roiling energy of an approaching storm mirrored the turmoil in his soul. He felt lost; adrift like a rudderless ship.

In the ten years since the reawakening, there seemed no place for a Great One. The war was over, the enemies sent away, or vanquished. The malicious damage they had done to the planet was reversed.

The people and animals had woken and emerged from the protected places, and returned to where their homes had been, to rebuild.

Before then, when the planet was still a desolate, polluted wasteland, he and his siblings had purpose. They were three minds, a combined entity of pure energy, wielding the power of the whole planet. They had removed the poisons, and restored the water, land and air to life.

His siblings, Tymos and Kryslie, were also Great Ones but they had found another role to play – back on Earth where they had been born and where the Elders had foreseen a need for them.

He, Llaimos, was stuck on Tymorea, and his siblings had ceded their status as Heir Designates to him. One day he would succeed his father as High King Governor, but he did not feel ready for that.

For a time, he had travelled with his father to reassure the common people that they had not been forgotten. Then, his presence had reassured the more nervous citizens, and given them direction.

Now the rebuilding was over and memories of the terrible war were fading. Life was almost back to normal.

The trouble was, he had virtually no idea of 'normal' life.

The ruling Triumvirate Governors, his father Tymoros, President Jono Reslic and the Science and Education controller, Xyron – would not give him directions. He outranked them now; he was God-touched…

He was bored.

Ten years ago, his sibs had neatly summed up his problem. He was a grown man who had experienced neither childhood nor adolescence. He had knowledge and skills, but he hadn't learnt them.

In that moment, in the Temple of Dira, in which the Guardians of Peace had matured him from child to man, the knowledge of generations of Governors had come to him. So too had come mastery of physical skills.

What he needed was a purpose - a task that only he could do.

The first fat, heavy drops of rain began to fall as a deafening crack of thunder shook the ground. Lightning began to flash from cloud to cloud and in jagged forks to the ground. The wind gusted with staggering force, bending the surrounding trees and snapping branches.

Llaimos looked up to the flashing sky and hoped to hear the voices of the Guardians. He raised both arms, oblivious to rain dripping down his arms into his sleeves and drenching his face. In his mind he thought to them, "How can I serve you now?"

All he heard was the rain pelting onto the permacrete flagstones. He lowered his arms, and let the precious water soak his hair and drip down his neck.

From nearby, even with the roar of the wind, he was aware of the scuffling of the silent ring of guards and sighed inwardly. It wasn't fair to them, staying out, now the rain had started. He could tell them to go, and they would, but only a short distance. They had their duty to perform, and their commander to obey. They were to protect the High King's Heir Designate. It was a complication that he was also a Great One.

With another sigh, he turned to walk towards the covered arcade between the now closed shops. He had come to the City of Dira, intending to continue to the Temple to meditate with the Elders during the Season of Storms. He had reached the open plaza and realised that the prospect of meditation was less than appealing.

His ears heard, beyond the sound of the heavy rain on the permacrete, a frantic voice calling a name. The voice grew louder and Llaimos sensed the seeker, although visibility was merely a few feet.

Someone bumped into him. The voice calling, "Jorge" changed to a yelp of fear as the guards grabbed the person so presumptuous as to touch him.

"Release her," Llaimos directed, in the exact tone that his father would have used.

To the young woman he asked, "What brings you out in this storm?"

Lightning flashed above him. In that instant, he saw the woman's mouth drop open, and then quickly snap shut. She recognised him. He expected the same inane drivel that all the girls used when they met him.

"Prince Llaimos?"

Another flash of lightning illuminated her. She had the light brown hair characteristic of commoners. However, only one young woman had ever called him Prince. Once the Governors had returned, he had been given a new title.

"Tarri?" he asked in amazement.

"I...didn't expect you to remember me," she admitted.

Llaimos sensed her embarrassment, though it warred with her immediate worry. "You were calling for someone," he prompted gently.

"Yes, one of my students. Jorge. He is thirteen, and I guess you know what boys that age are like – into everything, interested in everything."

Llaimos realised with a pang that he didn't know. He had never been thirteen. However, he knew exactly what his father would do.

"Guardsman, assign half your squad to search for the boy. If he has sense, he will be cowering out of the rain."

The irony of his statement was not lost on him. Amusement intruded. He was a Great One - no one was going to question his choices or call him crazy for standing in the rain.

He directed Tarri to the shelter of the roof overhanging the door of a shop.

"Wait here, let the guards search."

"No, he is my responsibility."

One of the remaining guards drew in a breath, "Lady, you are talking to a Great One, you don't…"

"Sedric, if it was your child that was missing would you want me to tell you not to look for him?"

"No, Great One, but…"

"Then help us look," Llaimos suggested mildly.

When Tarri would have returned into the torrential rain, Llaimos held her arm and said quietly, "Wait a moment."

He let his mind search around for a trace of the boy's thoughts. He heard and put aside the thoughts of wet and cold from his guards, for they were stoically doing their duty. Finally he found one that was cold, wet, hungry and lost. He directed a guard to the place he sensed the boy to be.

Later, after Jorge was asleep, impressed into obedience by the concern and advice of a Great One, Llaimos and Tarri were alone – except for the ever-present guards.

"So you took my sister's advice and went to the city to learn," Llaimos remarked into a sudden silence, that was punctuated with thunder.

"Yes, though my mother wants me marry and give her more grandchildren," Tarri admitted.

Llaimos could empathise with her. He knew the Elders all believed he should marry and begin producing heirs to ensure continuation of his line. Only his being a Great One silenced their advice.

The thought of the necessary process was discomforting. He wasn't ready.

He realised then that he no longer seemed to feel the storm within him, or the impatience, the boredom, the lack of direction.

Here was a woman who would talk to him as an equal, was intelligent, capable, and doing work that mattered to her. He didn't find it strange that she didn't just want to be a mother and stay at home.

As he talked, and learnt more about what was important to her, he realised that she was like him in believing there was more to life than what she had known growing up. She was doing something more – bringing higher education to children in the smaller towns and villages – to bright intelligent youngsters who might otherwise be stifled in a life of farming or herding or mining.

Something inside him relaxed. For the first time that he could recall – he felt at peace.

He realised with a shock equal to a clap of thunder that he had been talking to this woman for hours, when he usually felt the urge to flee when girls were presented to him.

It was as his father had said – "There is a season and a time for every purpose".

"Tarri, I know this is sudden, but would you consider being my consort? Would you let me help you with your work?"

"But…you're a Great One…"

"There isn't much call for a Great One these days."

"You are your father's heir…"

"One who knows all he does. Personally, I hope he lives for decades more."

"I'd have to live in the palace…"

"Why would that be a problem?"

"Because all the men think I am not doing a woman's job."

"My father would tell you it is important work."

"No man has wanted to marry me because…"

"You are better than they are. And you are wrong about the palace…there are many strong willed women doing worthwhile jobs there. Or do you think my sister was some kind of court decoration?"

Tarri recalled meeting his sister and had to agree – she had a mind of her own.

Instead, she glanced at the guards.

Llaimos had long ago learnt to ignore them.

"We don't have to live at the palace and I can tell President Governor Reslic to instruct the guards to vanish. That is an advantage of my fancy title. I just hadn't seen a reason to make an issue of things until now."

Tarri considered his question for a long while before answering.

"Yes," she said finally. "You are like no other man I have met. I will be your consort. But I don't want to have babies right away."

It came out like a challenge, but Llaimos smiled with relief.

"Not until we are ready – when the season is right," he agreed.

A brilliant flash of lightning lit the garden outside and lingered perceptibly. Llaimos felt a brush of the Guardians, like a gentle breeze ruffling his hair and a hint of tinkling voices. Perhaps they had sent little Jorge to show him what had been there all along - to open his eyes to the gift they had kept for him.

He sent them his thanks.

Bearly Spring

David Berry

I'm so hungry I could eat you. Well at least the snow and ice has gone: spring has sprung.

I'm pretty thirsty too, sleeping through winter is great, and, you miss all those rubbish repeats on T.V., except of course that ace program Yogi Bear; he's not as big as me, but a pretend bear. Wish I had a telly.

I'm just coming out of hibernation. No, that's not part of the United Nations, just what we bears do in spring.

What we bears do all spring, summer and fall, is eat, eat, eat. We have a really big feed up when we wake up so we can get through our next hibernation.

In spring there's always loads of new foliage to eat: new grass, my first taste of honey. I love honey, but hate those pesky bees. All I do is take what they're supposed to do — make honey. There's one of me with a massive appetite and thousands of them, and all they have to do is get the nectar, make my honey and keep one lady happy — how hard is that?

Who needs a winter fuel allowance? Do like I do and sleep through it.

One thing this hibernation thing does is play havoc with my arthritis. My joints get pretty stiff in this cave. Weeks sleeping, then wham, wake up thirsty, starving, and you're supposed to be up and running in minutes. After all, I can't ring for a kebab or Indian takeaway can I?

My cousin Pollaxe is a polar bear in the Arctic; they never hibernate. He doesn't bother with all this hibernation rubbish, nor does my cousin Specky. He's a spectacled bear and lives where it's warm so he doesn't have to hibernate because he's a lucky so-and-so and can eat any time.

Here's a spring song for you. When it's spring again, I'll bring again, etc. etc. Question is, what's for breakfast? Blimey, all this spring air makes you quite giddy, but guess what, I'm sure ready for a bath.

Now what's my springtime favourite, good for the bowels? Some lovely, tasty, broad leaf plants, and new grass. A bit like you eating your breakfast fibre. I eat loads of these leaves.

They're yummy, but not very filling, so it's onto my first taste of honey. We bears need to eat loads in Spring, Summer and fall; bulk out if you will, for the Winter.

I also love herbs, which are ready to eat; later berries and nuts which come in summer and fall.

After winter, you always get carcasses of animals which haven't survived the elements - deer, elks. Very tasty and no chasing.

Lovely breakfast; now for a mid-morning snooze in the lovely spring sunshine. Montana is a lovely place to live. Mountains, forest, rivers. What more do you need?

Well, that was a lovely snooze, but now for elevenses.

All those lovely tourists come here. They're scared to death of us so lots of yummy free food for this mid-morning treat; oranges, apples, bananas and peanut butter sandwiches. I don't have to dig for grubs, just tasty free food. Thank you tourists.

This beautiful spring day has made me sleepy again. Save my energy before my favourite time of day: lunch time and a bath — wonderful.

Forty winks and off to the rushing Montana river, melting ice, lovely cool, cool water to wash my bits. After all, it's coming round to the love season too.

Crayfish, frogs, molluscs and snails for starters, then a few birds' eggs. Tight I know, but they can lay more tomorrow. My babies take months; I love my first tree climb and admire my beautiful homeland — plus, free eggs. Result?

Look, I can see my first snowshoe hare. Is it my fault he's no longer white. What I don't understand is why does he freeze when he sees me? But he was tasty. I love my life in Montana, especially springtime. New life, new adventures, and plenty from God's bounty.

Now for bath time. I have this favourite rock I sit on because it's covered in a type of lichen, which is a bit rough, but great for exfoliating. But before this, I'm off to my scratch tree. You know when you get that itchy back just where you can't reach? Here goes. Oh my goodness, such bliss. I've wanted to do this for weeks, left a bit, right a bit, down, down.

Oh, just there — heaven.

I use my scratch tree to get the mites to the surface then wham, water at one degree does the trick, and just to be sure a rub on my favourite rock clears them out of my other regions. I use a sandy pebble for the other bits.

Now for my dip, give it the old toe first. Oh, that's cold, very cold, but here goes, my spectacular belly flop in Montana's best fast flowing mountain river. Burrrrrr, cold, but wonderful.

Well back to this lovely spring sunshine to dry off, and then a leisurely walk through all the gorgeous spring flowers to perfume my bits.

This is only a practice run for later in the summer when the love stuff comes around again.

Petunia, Marigold, Tulip. That's my pet names for my favourite lady bear. She doesn't realise it shortens to PMT, but come on, she can be moody. Once a year! It should be me who's moody. Meet once a year, have some fun, then eat more tourist cake, how good is that?

Well first day of spring over. Tomorrow I'm going on my first real food forage. Best not to push it with the Rangers, they can get upset if I frighten the tourists. When I see them, they'll give me my annual check-up. I get a dart in my bum, but I don't mind. They cut my nails, check my teeth, and give me a, well man bear check-up.

Now, what's for tea?

The Rites of Spring

Arthur Ives

The days lengthened and the warmth of spring replaced the cold, blustery, winter conditions. She marvelled at life's miracles. Chicks cheeped beside their opened tombs, lambs frisked, calves frolicked and foals staggered to their feet. From the soil's surface, bulbs, plants and weeds in their millions appeared. Her broad beans flowered, formed and filled. This was her first edible crop.

Life was on the march.

After daylight each morning, whatever the weather, she would wander about as if she were in the Garden of Eden. Neither Adam nor Eve could have been more conscious of the world's wonder than she.

Throughout her life she had watched, fascinated, as the cycle of life unfolded - from the first flirtations between the sexes to the mating, from the mating to the fulfilment of new birth, from new birth to the nourishing, on and on. The urge, imperative, instinctive, without exception. The drive unconscionable - the desire so overpowering that fights to the death were common.

She needed to help found a new generation. It was more than love. She had to mother a child. All the calls for great endeavours, even to see her present dreams realised, shrank, replaced by that goal.

It was time to marry her man.

Spring

Margaret Taylor

So happy are we now spring is here;
The very first season of the year.
Bluebells and daffodils, spring flowers galore,
Are spread all over nature's floor.
Baby birds hatch high up in their nest,
Hedgehogs stretch out and wake from their rest.
Young lambs frolic in fields all around,
Baby rabbits hidden under the ground.
Now is so good a time to be alive,
To see plants and animals really thrive;
The miracle of nature for all to share,
Is spread over the earth everywhere.
Parents' heads held high with pride,
As they see their daughter become a bride.
Friends and family share their joy,
As she becomes joined to her special boy.
Everything's new in this season of spring,
The flowers, the trees; yes everything.
We sit and wonder, and even treasure,
Why this time of year gives so much pleasure.

Spring Song

Rita Hodgson

The sun rises earlier, now,
Out of my glory box come garments
Folded away at the end of last summer
Stored in darkness
Awaiting the turning of the year.

Where the silver fish have feasted
I sit with needle and silks
Working the holes into a border of flowers.
Then, in my finery, I can join the other blossoms
In the exuberance of Spring.

Objects In The Rear View Mirror

Seem Closer Than They Really Are

Carol Cooper

Time
Time catches
Time catches up
Time catches up with
Time catches up with us.
Well when I've passed my exams
Now when I've earned enough I'll....
Do that trip one day
When I win the lottery
Then I'll go away.
Then I'll do that frippery
Beneath the frangipani tree
See the pyramid stand tall
See the thunder of the water fall.
They are very clear
In the rear view mirror.
Time catches up with us
Time catches up with
Time catches up
Time catches
Time.

Four Seasons? Totally Confusing.

Brian Croft

Spring, Summer, Autumn and Winter: there they are, the four different times of year which individually influence the way that we live. So much of what we do is affected by these climatic capsules and we adjust to each of them depending upon the calendar.

The clock times get altered back and forward, the shops stock different items, sales times in the large stores are set according to the presumption of good or bad weather, holidays are defined by the same yardstick and schools and universities are affected as well as sports and pastimes. (My mother in law's temper was an exception. This had only one season and it was constant!)

But, is it real? Are there actually four seasons? In reality we find that Spring merges into Summer, and Summer merges into Autumn and likewise Autumn into Winter and Winter into Spring. It's all very confusing and should we not look upon our climate as having one varying weather pattern and forget all about this season system created by man?

It becomes even more mixed up as we cross the world. Many countries have two seasons; one Dry and one Wet. Indeed, the extreme ends of the earth may be said to have one season which varies slightly through the year.

If we didn't have a "First day of Spring" or the "Last day of Summer" would it make any difference?

Australia is a particular example. Presumably, Adelaide and Ayers Rock must work to different systems and Darwin and Melbourne may well be totally at odds.

All this becomes even more confused when we compare the Northern and

Southern hemispheres. Our Winter may be New Zealand's summer and our so-called Spring may be their Autumn and the Kalahari will just be having a very dry season.

I find all of this confusing. How about you? Which idiot designated four seasons in the first place!!!?

Hope you keep warm this "Winter".

Spring Rains

Rita Hodgson

Winter had been long, cold, dry,
And like ancient skin
The land was parched and wrinkled.

Grass had become sere,
Fallen leaves skeletal,
Dust was everywhere,
Raised by wintry winds.

Then the rains started.
First, mist drifted in,
Clouds and fog filled the valleys,
Gentle, almost absent-minded.

You could hardly call it rain,
Scotch mist perhaps,
Just enough to settle the dust.

The earth, like a woman,
Began to primp a little.
Her complexion got better
Wrinkles plumping out
Tresses newly coloured.

Trees and bushes drank in the spring
Daintily put out buds and new shoots,

Four Seasons
Birds began to talk
Of nests and eggs
and rehydrated worms.

Still the rain fell
Heavier now, and warmer,
Setting the streams to chuckling,

Until at last,
The earth was moist, soft
Sated.

The rain stopped
Peace now, and an expectant pause.

Then the clouds parted to let the sun
Gild the raindrops
On the opening buds.

Spring Forward

Amanda Lacey

Spring Forward! Banish monotonous winter
With its greyness, drabness and grumpy impatience!
Emerge from the womb, ripened and flourish
Free at last from your monochrome cocoon.

Spread seeds of vibrant colour over desolate landscapes,
In a metamorphosis of bright
Diverse forms, each beautiful in its essence.

Bring fun, flirtation and laughter exampled by birds
Who dance and sing, displaying their feathery bling.

Intensify the sun bathing sodden ground,
Evoking your perfumes to awaken creatures in
Search for plump fruits amidst a floral eruption.

Let them join the comedy festival as
Serotonin washes away ill humour
And infernal night is exiled to the extremities.

Enticed by the promise of warmer dazzling days,
New beginnings are welcomed with a buzz,
Compelled to continually grow and blossom.

Spring into Action!

Elio Baldan

Foolish and frivolous moments are irresistible, and though at times irrational, they act as a trigger to a prickly escape because everything else around us seems stale and lifeless. So get hold of any excuse to sing your own praises, seize those moments with open arms and then stare ahead with starry eyes.

'Spring into action!' We hear the encouragement arriving from everywhere and so enticing to send us in the rain that a moment earlier was totally unexpected.

Now that winter has been left behind and frost is no longer a threat to new buds, the blossoms appear in great clouds of white, yellow, pink and at times in a combination of colours we are tested to describe. And leaves galore! Tender and green, to then age gracefully in the following months and finally turn an alluring red. The autumn winds will tear them down, falling in mounds that will quickly grow into knolls. And watching it happen will announce the transformation of an ever recurring event filled with precious moments.

It was early spring when I first saw her. Not face to face... oh, no! I was too shy and undeserving to expect an encouraging sign. But the path was narrow and I didn't think walking behind her would assist me in any way. My mind had resolve, so I made sure my shoes pounded the pavement with the greatest of results, and as I went past I summoned whatever amount of courage I could muster and dared say: "Hi!" This was the shortest invocation I had ever made.

So here it was: the frivolous moment fate had offered. So fleeting yet so appropriate... even though awkward.

She said nothing, and I could not think of anything else to say. In two minds whether to stare back at her hoping to demonstrate my cool charm or swiftly disappear down the deepest hole imaginable. There, in front of me and growing deeper!

But it was Spring, the smell in the air carrying the perfume of the season, and birds were busily chirping as if to say –go home young man, you've already done enough to leave a mark in her mind.

I ran the rest of the way, anxious to get home and fill an entire page in my diary, adding things to make the encounter exciting and definitely more successful. My infatuation was rekindled in a way to feel the heat, everything happening within the perfume of roses and my mind abuzz with the frivolity of springtime.

Spring is Here

Rita Hodgson

Turn off the heat, and lift up the blinds!
Open the windows and let in the spring!
Fingers of sunlight find dusty corners,
And suddenly the need for renewal is strong.
Weed the garden! Spring clean the house!
And don't forget the attic room
Marked 'Memories'!

Old pictures of people and places –
Travel brochures from journeys long done,
Not needed – wanted,
Part of our past.
Good enough to keep!

Yet each year some need a good clean –
Pockets full of sorrow and resentment,
Finery tarnished with tears
Choices made and regretted,
Feet of clay discovered too late,

If memories hurt, we need to say 'thank you',
Accept, forgive, move on,
Gather up all the blame and guilt,
And light a bonfire!
Then fold the gentled remains away
Into the drawer marked 'Lessons Learned'.

This spring I shall formally discard
My sackcloth and ashes,
Turn over a new leaf in my book of songs,
Dress myself for summer,
And dance!

The Four Seasons

Peter Gray

Sun is rising as I stir from my rest
From my bed, I rise with zest
Blurry eyes look out of my room
But in the sky, no dark clouds loom
Spring's fragrant scent is in the air
All new buds are bursting out there
Days filled with a warm sunny glow
Occasional rain to make gardens grow

Holiday time, families going away
Sun streaming down, while children play
The barbeque sizzles, smoke swirls around
Sausage and steak on the grill abound
It's a thirsty time at the picnic spot
Of cola and beer there's always a lot
Hot summer winds, gust and blow
Whipping up dust storms, as they go

Convertibles, cabriolets with hoods folded down
All day long they've been driving around
Balmy days and nights so fine
Now it's alfresco, we like to dine
Autumn's the time that I like best
As slowly the sun sets in the west
The weather has settled and all is calm
And now my country shows its charm

Wintery clouds over head is a sign
Not much longer will the warm sun shine
Each day shorter than the one before
Temperatures dropping, that's for sure
No more blazing wood fires of old
Too much trouble, and pollution we're told
Howling winds and soaking rain
I can't wait, till spring's here again.

Summer

Summer

Margaret Taylor

The trees abundant with bright green leaves,
That gently shimmer in the summer breeze.
People wander around country parks,
Gleefully watching the hovering skylarks.
Garden parties celebrated on the lawn,
Gatherings that last from dusk till dawn;
Everyone outdoors for many an hour,
Hoping there's no chance of a summer shower.
Flowers all out in brilliant full bloom,
Casting away memories of winter gloom;
Days much longer, nights so light,
All the flowers facing the sun so bright.
Youngsters stroll down lovers lane,
Caring not for the summer rain,
Sharing their evening of stolen bliss;
Sealing their love with a lingering kiss.
Everyone loves the long summer days,
At home or abroad in their own happy ways.
Yes we all have a very special reason
For loving this amazing summer season.

June, Lake Cascade, Idaho

From The Cloven Pine

D Garrett Nadeau

The sky bristled grey, moving like the hairs on a running wolf's back, the air wilful with fine drizzle. The trees around us creaked and groaned in the haze, and relentless, the lake licked the shore. We sat close up to the fire on the logs we'd placed there. We'd put on our dark green ponchos, hoods up, and the mist droplets stippled and glistened, then ran down in little rivulets of crystal. I let Ranger Clay chat as he cooked.

He seemed in a good mood despite the change in the weather and talked about something called 'symbiosis' which he defined as 'different creatures living together.' He said in part it was about evolution like the way flowers had developed over time with the help of insects. He talked about hermit crabs and the shells they adopt and parasites like fleas that live off their host. He asked did I know that almost half of all living creatures on this Earth had at least one parasitic phase in their life? And he said there was a bird in Egypt that sits in a crocodile's mouth and cleans the croc's teeth. And there were fish that swim with sharks that sanitise the shark's skin and feed on bits of food floating off the shark's latest catch. 'We all need each other for something,' he said. 'Why else are we here?' And he took a pipe out of an inner shirt pocket, filled it from a pouch out of his jacket, and lit it. I suppose it was a break from chewing tobacco.

It all sounded wonderful, complementary and fine, but the Nature that hovered not five yards away, surrounding us on all sides, harsh and indifferent, had no mind to co-operate. I poked the fire with a stick, a mixture of annoyance and confusion churning up inside me. I picked up my History notebook that had been lying there on the ground getting wet. I opened the cover and fanned the pages. There was nothing in it to indicate it had even been opened. I was feeling defiant and careless of its exposure to the thin rain. I determined a confrontation was long overdue, and set myself to meet Ranger Clay's gaze eye to eye. 'Ranger Clay, when do you think somebody's going to tell me straight what's going on?'

Looking at me grey-eyed, steady, he didn't seem at all phased by the question. He drew a couple of puffs on his pipe. 'Well, to start off with it ain't up to me. Thar's others involved.' He sucked on the pipe again, hard, to prevent it going out. The tobacco glowed and puffs of smoke sprang out of the side of his mouth. 'It's a matter, too, of knowing who to trust. And that don't mean we don't trust you. It's a whole lot more complicated than that. There have been disagreements, you see – among ourselves. About what to do, what's expected of us. About whether to involve you – some think we shouldn't - for your own protection.' He paused, taking the pipe out of his mouth, holding it up like it needed to be inspected, then putting it back in his mouth all the while the wet breeze sliding through the trees and us listening as if we were supposed to believe it, too, was advising caution. 'You see, we ain't sure ourselves what's goin' on. You know, we ain't even certain what to think. Hell, thar's one or two deems this is all some sort of mass hallucination, or some mind control experiment by the military – some trick like that. Or, just someone masquerading, playing a joke on all of us. But we have this kind of really strong sense of needing to be cautious – a sense that don't even feel like it comes from ourselves. Does that sound a bit strange?' He looked at me steady, sincere, genuine. He worked his mouth, puffing again on his pipe, then answered his own question. 'Yep, I suppose it does.'

'Who's "us"?'

He worked the pipe in his mouth from side to side, thinking. 'It's not up to me to tell you that. For now, it's a pretty small group. Listen, Conrad, all I can say is that sometimes it's like we all get certain feelings – all of us at the same time. It frightens us – sometimes - even the strongest among us. But we're being careful - about acting on those feelings. We can manage them – for now at least, well, most of us anyway. But don't get me wrong – they ain't bad feelings. Just the opposite most of the time. I can't really say more than that – except, of course, that one feeling is that you need to be involved. But we don't know how or why. And we don't know if it's safe. So, we're taking it slow, trying to handle what's going on. Though I personally ain't so sure we can. Believe it or not, we're trying not to frighten you.' He attempted a smile. 'How we doin'?'

In the uneasy breeze, the fire flicked back and forth like it was trying to escape the logs that held it, and the thin sleet hissed in the coals like a burning, diamond snake and twisted round us as if it was aiming to elevate right up into our faces, hissing and hinting at tragedies that no one could predict or prevent. 'I'm not scared, I said, '– if that's what you're asking.' But he had hit on something, something I hadn't fully realised myself. 'It's funny though,' I said, '- what you just said about feelings. I hadn't thought about it, but it's like I've been getting certain emotions, too – from somewhere out there.' I looked out and away from under the dripping hood of my poncho and held up my hand to the drizzle-drenched forest. 'Like from somewhere hidden and dense. They aren't really from inside me at all.' I hesitated, trying to make a more certain determination. 'One of those, of course, is that I'm not really supposed to be afraid. So, no, I'm not scared, not at all.' I realised then what he meant about the uncertainty. I was glad though to be talking to someone about what I'd been feeling.

The wind stilled like a frightened colt not knowing which way to turn, then reared up again. Ranger Clay clutched the pipe from his mouth, downfaced it by the bulb, and tapped it hard against his log to empty it. 'Well, I reckon that's a good thing, Conrad, son – you not being scared.' But when he looked up at me again his eyes told me he was being more encouraging with his words than certain with his thoughts.

A Period of Refreshment

Carol Cooper

Martin was rather miffed when his wife, Claire, arranged a holiday in Venice with a group of friends. "Venice", Claire had told them, was "not Martin's cup of tea, or rather coffee", she added as they leafed through holiday brochures.

"He grumbled about being charged a king's ransom for coffee in St. Mark's Square. There we were, listening to an orchestra in one of the most famous cities in the world, and all he could do was moan!" Claire was looking forward to renewing the experience – sans Martin.

Martin, however, was determined not to be eluded completely. Leafing through one of the brochures Claire had left on the coffee table, he discovered a culinary experience holiday in Venice on the same week Claire had booked for her trip.

Logging on to Google, he discovered that his hotel was only a hundred yards or so from the hotel in which Claire was staying. Martin's holiday would involve mornings spent cooking, or watching others cook, with a few trips to local food markets. Evenings were reserved for trips to sample the local cuisine in various restaurants. Afternoons were free.

Martin booked his place, and a flight later in the day than Claire's. He meant to surprise her by walking into her hotel on the first evening (free on his itinerary) wearing his secret, recent acquisitions; a straw Panama, and designer shades. He would strike the right air of casual sophistication and world-wise 'cool'. Yes, he was, he really was, ready for an adventure!

Flight of Fancy?

Assuming all the innocence his round and rather silly face could muster, he saw Claire off at the airport. Soon his own flight was called and he enjoyed it immensely. He was seated beside a very attractive French woman who assured him that she was booked onto the same holiday as himself. Life for Martin took on a rosier hue.

Vive La France

Valerie was her name. She suggested to Martin that, as they were both there as singles, perhaps he would join her at the hotel bar that evening for the introductory speech and drinks put on by the holiday facilitator? Martin hesitated. He should carry out his plan to surprise Claire; on the other hand he ought to make an effort to mingle.

Valerie had loads of coquettish charm. She seated herself on a high bar stool, her head held a little to one side, waiting for his answer.

"Mais, bien sûr, Madame", said Martin scraping together some phrase-book French. Valerie replied in French – but he didn't quite catch that bit.

The Start Of An Affair

So it came about that Martin did not surprise Claire that evening, but did he surprise Valerie? Dear reader, think what you will about that evening – Honi soit qui mal y pense.

Venice has its magic, especially in the evenings when the trippers have departed – but Aspetta! What of Claire? She was enjoying a boozy evening with the girls. The group attracted several local male admirers, eager to make the acquaintance of women without partners, women out to recapture their lost youth.

The Way We Were

So it happened that Claire and Martin had not met by the middle of the week, yet the two of them boarded the same busy ferry to see the glass blowers at Murano. Martin was squiring Valerie, while Claire was escorted by an attentive and elegant Rosanno Brazzi look-alike. This could have proved awkward. Both Claire and Martin each saw the other at the same time. Claire looked stunned, while Martin felt his face reddening. Claire was so shocked she didn't notice Valerie, and Martin was too busy making explanations for his appearance in Venice to give Rosanno even a passing glance.

Both Valerie and Rosanno were quick and discreet. They melted easily into the crowd. After all they were old hands at holiday romances.

"What happens in Venice, stays in Venice", or home where the heart is.

Claire and Martin enjoyed their excursion to Murano; but then went back to their respective hotels to finish their week as they had planned. Claire enjoyed the orchestra in Piazza San Marco, and Martin enjoyed his cucina Italiana. They even took their scheduled - and therefore separate - flights home.

Venice had been an interesting interlude – but not a damaging one. Indeed, truth to tell, they both found it to be a period of refreshment.

Sweet Surrender

Linda Ann Ford

Ah, to while away the summer days,
lost in sweet surrender.
To be one with all of nature,
as my mind turns to wander.
There within my fantasies,
my heart will find delight.
Everything around me,
is perfect in my sight.
The earth is blanketed in green,
and flowers' sprinkled hues.
Every day a paradise,
with nothing I must do.
The melodies within my soul,
play out their silent tune,
and I am lost to rapture,
on a summer's afternoon.

Summer of '70 Point Duty

David Berry

Only one week had passed since I had been posted to my first station, Accrington Police Office. What a week — sunny, warm and life felt so good.

After a hard and gruelling 16 weeks training, suddenly I was there, my first ever real posting. During our course, it had been a long hot spell way back in 1970, all the marching, studying, rugby games against a bunch of gorillas from the Welsh forces. I think I still have bruises to prove it.

Then there was the famous "ramsamies". For those wondering, that meant a monthly concert at the police training centre at Warrington. Each class had to perform in front of all the students and instructors and THE COMMANDANT. They called it character building. Some great singers, Liverpudlian comedians, a Welsh choir, dancers, and a very bendy, totally gorgeous lady escapologist (what she was doing in the police baffled us). And then there was N class, us.

We had decided to do a song and dance routine which sadly for us, the management, i.e. the Commandant, wasn't quite ready for, and we were ordered off the stage mid act, but we didn't care, the students loved it.

Enough of that, back to my first posting:

Monday 6th July 1970, 8 a.m., first day at my new station. A quick station tour, introductions to other colleagues, and my new sergeant, Bill Simmons PS 1673.

After a short chat he said, "Go and get a drink in the canteen, then come back here."

"Yes Sergeant."

At 9.30, I went back to the Sergeant's office.

As soon as I entered the office, Sergeant Simmons said, "PC 2372, we've got your first job, a sudden death. PC Douglas will take you to the address, listen to what he tells you and learn. There's the address."

PC Douglas took me out to the car and said, "It's Tommy by the way".

He looked old, but somehow I just felt this aura around him, a halo of wisdom you could say. I felt safe with him. He was quiet in the car and didn't say anything about what I was about to face.

Can you imagine the shock and trepidation I felt when we arrived at the house some three minutes from the station? We were greeted by two newly married teenagers.

My immediate thoughts were; it must be Mum or Dad, but no. They asked us to come upstairs with them, they were both sobbing uncontrollably, and they took us upstairs to their bedroom.

By now, I was shaking, and Tommy said reassuringly, "Keep calm lad, I'm 'ere to 'elp thi."

Then my heart sank to a point I'd never experienced before in my life.

"She's there", the young man said. I looked down into the cot and saw a tiny baby, a 3-month-old girl. I was mortified.

The ambulance crew arrived and came upstairs. One of them was Bob Gibson, my best mate. He'd only been in the ambulance one month. Tommy said to them, "Can you have a look at the baby lads?"

They confirmed that she was dead.

Tommy then asked them to take the young couple downstairs and asked Bob to make the tea. But before they could move, I said, "What's your names please, and the baby's name?"

"I'm Andy, this is Susan, my wife, and our baby is called Suzie."

I thanked the young man and said, "Andy, give details to the ambulance men when you get downstairs, thanks."

When they left the room, Tommy said, "Tha needs ta check the baby now lad."

With great reluctance, I thought to myself, I have to do this for all their sakes. I picked up the baby and said, "Hello Suzie."

To this day I don't know why. She was still warm and felt really heavy. I can't describe how empty I felt at that moment. I must confess, I had wondered at that point, why Tommy had asked me to check the baby, but I knew he'd have an answer later.

The ambulance then took the baby and the parents to Accrington Victoria Hospital (AVH) and the baby was then confirmed dead.

Monday 10.15am, 6th July 1970 is etched on my heart.

Tommy then said, "Come on lad off to AVH. No training can ever prepare you for this."

At Warrington, we had filled the forms, asked the questions, but Suzie was real. We had to contact the coroner at the hospital and he said, "Post Mortem here at 2.45pm."

Those words made me shiver. Post Mortems are real, not textbook stuff.

We left the hospital and went back to the station. On the way back, I said to Tommy, "Why did I have to check the baby, when she was already dead?"

Tommy to my amazement replied, "Ah lad, PC2372, people do murder their children ya know lad."

That had never even entered my head, Tommy then said, "Tek it from me lad, all deaths are suspicious till somebody tells thi different."

I never forgot that advice.

Tommy said, "Some things are harder than others, lad. I've done this job for twenty year, and when it's flippers it's even harder. Come on, I'll get thi a brew at the nick."

We just had time to drink it when I got a radio message. "PC 2372, make your way with PC Douglas to a fight at the corner cafe on Peel Street."

"Roger Wilco."

Off out to the Panda, me expecting blue lights, Starsky and Hutch handbrake skids. No, not Tommy, a nice steady drive to Peel Street cafe. On the way, Tommy said, "Its bloody hot weather lad, they all go crackers when it's 'ot."

Adrenaline pumping, me itchin' to get stuck in, but just as I was about to dive out of the Panda, Tommy said, "Whoa, whoa lad, led 'em feit. They calm down when they see us."

So behind Tommy into the cafe and Tommy said, "Hey Culshaw, pack it in. Why you feiting wi' thi Dad?"

Tommy, much to my amazement, then said, "It's your DAD when all sed and done. Tha shouldn't be feiting with thi DAD! Billy what ya doin' feiting?"

"Sorry Tommy," said Billy, the Dad, "I'm going now, dornd lock mi up will thi."

Tommy said, "What does ti say Jack?"

Jack owned the cafe. He said, "I can't weigh'em up Tom. Father and son fighting. Tell 'em off Tom, but they 'av to pay for mi cups and tae."

Tommy said, "Pay up or yer banged up both of ya."

Billy paid and Tommy said to them, "Now bugger off and behave your bloody self."

I was gob-smacked. Judge and Jury I thought, fight resolved, damage paid, sentence passed. I did learn there's more to this career than textbooks.

After refs at the station - refs means meal break time - you get 45 minutes if you're lucky. Then I had my first post mortem on a three-month-old baby girl. The pathologist was brilliant with me; he explained everything he had to do, even on this very tiny baby.

We had to weigh the baby's organs and I must admit I was fascinated by their weight and how big they were in this tiny baby. He wrote out a form as to her cause of death and this was pulmonary obstruction due to bronchial pneumonia. Five p.m., the end of a very emotional day.

Tommy said, "Well done lad, am proud of thi."

Tuesday, 8 a.m. start, still this amazing summer weather.

Sergeant Simmons was waiting for me and said, "Your first patrol this morning on town centre beat 2. You'll be working with PC 437 Hubbard (sadly now deceased), he's been with us a month."

So off to the town centre with PC Hubbard, (John), me feeling very important in shirt sleeve order, radio, handcuffs, truncheon, a proper policeman.

When John said, "I'll show you my street plan I've made over the past three months. This is Church Street and at the end of the road is the A680, the main road to Blackburn, that's called Blackburn Road."

I thought to myself, I know where I am, I'm from Ossy, so I said, "John I'm from Ossy. I know where I am."

"Oh great," said John. "I'm from Bury, so I need a street plan. In that case, I'll show you round the brew shops and stuff you should know then you can go on TC 2 (town centre patrol) on your own for a bit if you want."

John took me around all the places you could get a brew and I remember thinking to myself, if I had a drink in all these places, I'd never get anything done, so I vowed then to only use them if I really needed to. I wanted to get on with being a bobby. We had refs at twelve. John spoke to Sergeant Simmons who said it was OK for me to go on TC 2 on my own for an hour.

John and I split up and off I went on TC 2. I was so excited and people asked me stuff like where's Eagle Street, can you tell me how to get to the hospital, etc. Simple stuff, but it made me feel very important.

Suddenly, the radio went, "2372 position."

At first I thought, what's that mean, then I realised they wanted to know where I was, so full of confidence, I replied, "2372 to control, Cannon Street."

A short, sharp rebuff came back.

"WHICH CONTROL? ACCRINGTON OR GREAT HARWOOD?"

Panic set in. I spluttered, "Accrington please."

PC Stevenson, the long tooth controller said, "2372, it's Accrington over, Sgt Simmons wants to see you in the Sergeant's office pronto."

"Roger over," was my choking reply. I legged it back to the office to be greeted by the ever-calm Sergeant Simmons.

"He's one for the radio protocol is PC Stevenson, listen and learn 2372."

"Yes, Sarge, is everything all right?"

"First of all 2372, this is not New York. Kindly address me as Sergeant Simmons, not Sarge, and secondly, yes everything is fine and very well done for yesterday. PC Douglas told me how well you had done under the circumstances, but today you're off on escort. Report to the charge office sergeant. He'll explain what you have to do."

"Yes Sergeant."

So off I went to the charge office to see Sergeant Norman.

Sergeant Norman truthfully wasn't the best example of a policeman. He was old and ready to retire, soup stained tie, etc. etc.

"Right young 2372, here's what you'll be doing, but first show me your handcuffs."

I took them out of my pocket (no special pouches then).

"Good lad, you're off to County Durham with a 16 year old. He's going to an approved school."

Here's the rules according to Sergeant Norman:

1. Never say yes to them.

2. Never give them anything.

3. Never take your eyes off them.

4. Finally, for God's sake, never trust them.

"This lad is an escaper, so when you handcuff, he stays handcuffed, got it?"

"Yes Sergeant Norman."

Off in the car with the civilian driver whose nickname was Captain Birds Eye, because he just looked like the fellow off the Birds Eye advert. It's a long journey to County Durham and Ken the driver at first didn't say much, but gradually he talked to me and I found out he was an ex-Regimental Sgt. Major in the army and a very sound guy.

He did say to me on the way, "One piece of advice for you PC 2372, never volunteer for anything and you'll survive." It was platinum advice.

I did feel a bit sorry for my charge. He'd had a crap life, no wonder he'd turned to crime. Then I added my own rule to the list:

5. Never get involved with your prisoner.

We arrived at the approved school about 5 o'clock. Ken said, "Ring the bell, take the cuffs off and we'll hang on to him, when the door opens, just stand back and let go."

"Why?"

"You'll see," said Ken.

I rang the bell, the door opened, stood back and wham. Our charges feet left the ground and he flew through the door.

Next thing, "What's your name?"

The lad said, "Anthony Thoms."

Next thing, whack, "Anthony Thoms, what?" came from the reception officer.

"SIR" quickly came from master Thoms.

Crisis over, Ken said, "That could have been you if you didn't stand back."

Laughing away he was.

10.30 p.m.: return to the nick. Long day, but another learning curve mastered I thought.

Wednesday: training day at Blackburn DHQ and interview with Chief Superintendent.

It went well as I had a good report from Bruch, Warrington (our training headquarters) and according to Sergeant Simmons, I had made a promising start. I was made up. Lunchtime, myself and three of my fellow trainees decided to nip to the pub across from DHQ for a nice cool shandy each.

However, me, Steve, Pam and Cheryl got a bollocking when we got back to class from Inspector Oddie (the wig), for drinking on duty. We tried to protest saying it was dinnertime, but that didn't work.

"You're always on duty when you're at work or at home. Remember that," was his advice, and he sternly said, "DON'T LET IT HAPPEN AGAIN, UNDERSTOOD?"

"Yes Sir," was our collective response. 5 o'clock finish, heaven.

Thursday, day off.

Friday was my first solo beat. Lovely, lovely day again. Sunny, gentle breeze and PC Berry released on an unsuspecting public TC 1 and 2. Two beats for me, then after an uneventful morning, afternoon my first ever process.

A motorist parked in the studs (not zigzags) of a pedestrian crossing. Just as I approached, the car driver returned to his car.

Eagle-eyed me noticed his tax had expired too and as he got in the car, his car moved before he did anything. I asked him to get out and pointed to the studs and the tax and said,

"Why did your car move? Did you have the handbrake on?"

He said, "IT DUN'T WORK."

Bingo I thought. I gave him an H.O.R.T. which in the full detail means Home Office Road Traffic form to produce his documents, but in my haste I actually forgot to ask him his name and address, gave him the form with Driving Licence, Insurance and Test accurately ticked, but no name and address. I immediately asked the sergeant if I could come in and complete my first process report and I got a yes.

When I got to the station, I looked at my H.O.R.T. And realised I hadn't got his name and address; ego deflated, tail and everything else between my legs and much to the amusement of the other PCs in the report room, I went to see the duty sergeant, Sergeant Clegg, who actually had the patience of Job said, "Think 2372, registration number ring a bell?"

Me: nothing. Zilch. Blankey, blank.

"Ring the vehicle licensing number at Preston, they'll help you solve your little problem," a very patient Sergeant Clegg said.

Problem solved, blushes gone, first report meticulously completed and handed in to Sergeant Clegg.

"Well done 2372, you resolved your little problem, but you missed a full stop on paragraph 6."

5 p.m., time to go home. A little deflated, but come on, my first process report. Exciting or what? Before I left, Sergeant Clegg said, "8 a.m. tomorrow 2372, don't be late."

As if - I couldn't wait. This was a Saturday. 8 a.m. Parade room. Ready for a very long shift. A sunny day in July, off to the lovely village of Whalley on point duty. How hard can that be?

Sergeant Simmons came in to brief me.

"Right 2372, 8.48 bus to Whalley Police Station and go and see Sergeant McKenzie. He'll explain what you have to do."

"OK Sergeant, thank you."

I was so chuffed, only 5 days gone and on the 6th day, off to help out at a new station. Can my career life get any better I thought?

Caught the bus at Melbourne Street, Accrington at 8.46am and off to Whalley. Driver dropped me outside Whalley Police Station at 8.30. Sergeant McKenzie let me into the station and guess what, Cheryl had been seconded from Blackburn for the day on traffic duty with me. How can it get better!!

Sergeant McKenzie explained to us how the weekend traffic system operates in Whalley centre then made us a drink as he lived at the public station. He told us it will be a long, hard day and said, "You'll be two hours on point duty, 30 minutes rest, 45 minutes for main refs: 2372 at 12 WPC 106 at 1 o'clock. He took us to Whalley centre, walked us around the one-way system then took us to our point.

The A59 ran through Whalley then; this was before the bypass. Sergeant McKenzie said, "2372, you go first for half an hour to get the feel of it, I'll bring 106 back at 9.30. She can do half an hour then you're on at 10 till 12. You two sure you've got it?"

"Yes sergeant," we replied.

9 o'clock and thought to myself, I can do this. The traffic at this point was light and easily manageable. Briefly how it had to work was traffic from Clitheroe had to turn left onto Accrington Road and the road was one way up to the junction of Princess Street. Traffic to Preston right lane, traffic to Accrington left lane.

Princess Street was also one way at weekends. Left lane Preston, right lane Clitheroe, as was George Street to its junction with Blackburn Road. Fool proof, eh!!

9.30 a.m., Sergeant McKenzie came back with PC 106 Cheryl. She took point; I went with the Sergeant to see all the one-way system. 9.45, I came back on point. Cheryl wasn't coping too well, but first time wasn't easy.

I was an HGV driver, used to the traffic. She was a student with little traffic experience. They teach you the hand signals at Warrington, but there's no actual traffic or worse still motorists to deal with. They can be a nightmare as I soon found out. Two hours waving your hands about was surprisingly tiring.

By 12 o'clock traffic had increased significantly and Cheryl was back to relieve me. She looked really uncomfortable so I decided not to go to the nick for my break and I stopped next to the launderette shop near to where she was.

As I stood there, my old boss from Trumix came out of the launderette and said, "Here you are David, some orange juice for you. You've got a hot, busy day to face yet." I was so chuffed, but acutely aware that Cheryl wasn't coping with the traffic which was building up very fast. HGVs, buses, cars, cyclists in their hundreds. The A59 is a very busy trunk road and this was a very busy July weekend.

At 12.30 I said to Cheryl, who then was only half an hour into her 2-hour traffic stint,

"Cheryl, stop all the traffic. I'll take over for you." The relief on her face could not have been measured in pounds, shillings and pennies. As she passed me, I said, "You go to the nick and tell Sergeant McKenzie you can't manage all the heavy traffic."

"OK Dave, thank you so much," she said.

Now for my challenge. All the traffic stopped, long, long queues in all directions so all the Preston traffic still stopped. I got the traffic moving towards Preston and

Clitheroe. Thank God it worked, just as Sergeant McKenzie appeared with Cheryl.

He asked if I was OK and said, "I'll get the Whalley PC to take over at 2. Will you be OK?"

"Yes thanks Sergeant."

And off he went with Cheryl.

2 o'clock and I got my 45-minute break. The Whalley PC did say sorry I was stuck on it so long, but to me the time just flew.

Back at 2.45, but trouble wasn't very far away. About 3.15, I saw a Volkswagen Beetle coming towards me from Preston. It had its right indicator on. I tried to wave it forward, but ominously the indicator stayed on.

I tried to wave the Volkswagen's lady driver forward, but she started to turn right and she hit me, causing me to fall forward onto the bonnet of the car and slide off onto the floor. It was a very slow impact.

I got up and said, "Did you not see me signalling you to go ahead?"

"I want to turn right," she said.

"It's a one way system, wait over there, I'll deal with you when I get relieved." She wasn't happy.

Five minutes after, the Whalley PC came back and took over the point so I could speak to my wayward motorist, but before I could, my ex-boss came out of the launderette with another drink and he said, "You look like you need this. I'm sorry about that. It's the wife driving one of the firm's cars. She usually only comes in the week to the shop so she's not used to the one way set up."

Now my predicament is free drinks for all the lads and
girls on traffic duty throughout the summer, ex-boss's
wife who made a silly mistake, bruised shin and ego for
me. So I thought about Tommy from Monday and the dad
and son and said to myself, David, your first dilemma, that
needs a decision, so I told her off, got a thank you from
her and my old boss, and kept the free drinks.

Back on point, PC 106 had been put in company with
the Whalley PC. She was happy, I was wiser and traffic
was getting better. Then 4.15 p.m., this car transporter
appeared from the direction of Preston.

As he got level with me, he asked how to get to
Accrington so I said, "As you pass me, get into the outside
lane and turn right at the next junction."

"OK thanks," he said, but neither of us realised that in
going into the outside lane, his right turn at the junction
would tighten the angle of his egress into Accrington Road
and as he rounded the corner, the cab of the HGV got
around OK, but the transporter bit didn't.

The car at the front of the transporter was over-hanging
to the nearside and struck the corner of a dress shop. Sand
slewed and nearly fell off the transporter. The bang told
me something else had happened, so I had to stop all the
traffic, and run up to the shop to see this car. I thought, oh
God, what do I do now?

Luckily for me, Sergeant McKenzie was just coming
out of the station 50 yards away. He called for traffic to
attend and brought 106 Cheryl with him. He told me to
reverse part of the one way and create a diversion route
and put PC 106 on point at that junction and then he told

me to go back to my point. We worked well together, me and Cheryl, her traffic fears gone. Traffic arrived and Cheryl heard him tell the truck driver to reverse the transporter.

106 coolly pointed out to him that the car would fall off if he did that. Quick change of plan by the traffic man and a suitable recovery vehicle was summoned. PC 106 got a pat on the back from Sergeant McKenzie and after 3 hours, the little village could breathe again.

Traffic system back to normal and two rookie PC's on their way home. I did tell Sergeant McKenzie about the Volkswagen incident and how I dealt with it and he said, "I admire your initiative, but always speak to your supervisor first. That way, someone else has made the decision, but well done anyway and thank you both for your hard work today."

I said my goodbyes to the lovely Cheryl, who gave me a hug. WHAT A WAY TO END OUR FIRST POINT DUTY DAY. 7.45 p.m., off back to Accrington to sign off.

The duty Sergeant asked, "Well, how did it go? In at the deep end or what 2372?"

So I just said, "Just my first summer point duty day Sergeant. It's been busy and eventful, and thankfully, at least I'm still alive."

Crosby Sands

Carol Cooper

One evening on Crosby Sands, I saw a girl put a sun hat on one of Gormley's expectant figures.

"I'm hoping it will be fine tomorrow," she explained, smilingly.

An empty beach. Lonely, yet full of peace and promise.

We watched the silver sand merge with the slate sky.

Marlborough Mansions

The silver-haired lady threw two gold rings into a skip outside her apartment. A tramp watched in surprise.

The lady turned to go in.

"You know they will bring you bad luck," she said, pausing by her open door. She went inside. The tramp swore.

Charlie Boy

The architect looked at London airport. It was like a souk.

Bad carpeting, low ceilings and flashy shops.

"I could design it better," he thought. "Light, airy - like they have abroad."

"Not all modern architecture is bad, Charlie boy," he chuckled when the new terminal at Heathrow was opened.

A Summer's Day

Rita Hodgson

We lay beneath sweat soaked sheets
Too hot to sleep.

Sunrise clawed the sky
With fiery talons.
The dusty north wind
Gusted from the desert
Making us catch our breath.

We sweltered.
No appetite, no energy
Prickly heat, prickly tempers,
Throughout that endless sultry day.

Even chilled champagne
Declined to fizz.

Finally the sun sank,
The wind dropped,
And the world stood still.

A few birds called –
Then dusk and silence,
Broken by the high pitched sound
Of marauding mosquitoes.

Two Continents
When I was younger,
I hoped to be thought
Smouldering and sultry.

I'm older now, and wiser.

Please, don't compare me
To a summer's day

Four Seasons

Arthur Ives

Few would not be moved by the great Vivaldi's transposition of the moods of 'The Four Seasons' into his violin concertos. Nor would many, on hearing random excerpts, fail to identify the particular season.

Springtime

If music can represent the seasons, so can the cycle of life. The season of spring takes me to the lengthening of days and the unfolding of the little miracles of life. Seeds sprout from pods, fields of flowers appear from dormant vegetation, and throughout the countryside, chicks hatch, calves frisk, lambs frolic, and foals find their feet. The cycle of life relentlessly progresses.

What else were the years from my birth to the time when I stopped fathering children, but the springtime of my life? Born in February 1926, seven years after the signing of the armistice between the Allies and Germany, I have now reached the autumn years, and, with nothing but gratitude for the four score plus seven years I have lived, I prepare myself mentally for the winter beyond.

What phenomenon in the universe's cycles causes the season of spring to visit us here in the southern hemisphere? Simply put, I'm told, it is an annual tilt in the earth's axis of rotation relative to the sun. Not only do days lengthen and warmth increase, but both of these stimulate growth, and provide an air of optimism and exhilaration.

How lucky I was to be born into the animal kingdom. How lucky, not to have been born a barnacle, or an aphid, or a blowfly, or a maggot. A simple human being. I had won one of life's greatest lotteries. Someone estimates that the chance of any one of us being conceived is one in 400 trillion – another suggests 700 trillion. So, back in 1926, there I was, born in the front bedroom of our home, the third boy to whom my mother had given separate births, in a shade over two years. Realising the drain each child makes on working class families, I wonder whether I came more as a burden than a blessing. Ahead of me, I had to learn all that was needed or required to know - how to survive physically, socially, academically.

The springtime of my life was the time for growth and development. Tentative at first, I strove to overcome the early inhibition of extreme shyness, and to make use of the level of gifts I had been allocated. But I felt that I was harnessed, more as a draught horse than one saddled from a bloodstock stable.

Occasional successes allowed me to sample the euphoria that the brightest and the best take for granted. Gardening was, and remains, a source of interest and satisfaction for me. At a gathering of the whole upper primary school when I was about ten, our headmaster, Mr Roberts, was giving a lesson on the earth's water cycle. He asked the class for the word that describes how water rises from the land and the sea to the clouds, and, because I'd learnt to disturb the garden's surface to stop the moisture escaping, I thought I might know that word. Timidly, I broke the silence. "Evaporation?" I suggested. Before acknowledging that I was right, he gave me an intense half smile, and I was able to anticipate his nod. For once, I went home from school, elated.

In spite of struggling with Latin, Physics and English, I left school with a reasonable pass. I began my working career in a job I detested. Nevertheless, I was glad that my school days were over. But learning? Never. I enrolled in many technical and correspondence schools that offered courses to help me in my work and leisure.

At school, I'd been a poor reader with little imagination and a miserable vocabulary. In an attempt to correct the situation, I made up my mind to become a reader, and to enlarge my understanding of words. Where to start? I'd heard of Homer, of Honeré de Balzac, of Victor Hugo, of Feodor Dostoevski, of Guy de Maupassant, and I ploughed into them. It's a wonder I persevered. I took a course in short story writing, and completed it satisfactorily. Of the decisions of a lifetime, the one to embrace literary pursuits was one of my best.

I approached adolescence as ignorant of the facts of life as if I'd been abandoned as a child on a deserted island. With embarrassing shyness, I admired the metamorphosis of plain schoolgirls into shapely young women, and despaired that I would ever share a close relationship with any one of them. Propinquity, the word that uniquely describes the proximity of one person to another, intervened, and, following a long and memorable courtship, I married a most attractive work mate, and we produced two adorable daughters.

Summertime

The springtime of my life merged into its summer, the time of pleasure, but also, of confrontation and trial. We'd become house-owners in suburbia, amassed a collection of needs for comfortable living, and I had found career contentment.

The tribulations of summer are in the troughs between the peaks of pleasure. Of the latter there are many - the moderate mornings and evenings, the delights of community get-togethers, the simple quenching of thirst, the lassitude of holidaying down by the sea or up in the cooler mountain air, the enjoyment of family. But we cannot overlook the hazards - droughts, fires, floods; wind, plagues and swarms; its storms of dust and rain. We faced these, never to extremes, but we did confront challenges that we might well have done without.

My career was centred in an organisation that pledged advancement and financial reward to conscientious and loyal team members. The higher company echelon preached these messages at every formal gathering. Because of the nature of the business my company was engaged in, when necessary, I worked ridiculously long hours. And also, because I was staff, there was no overtime payment. As my career progressed, I uprooted my family and relocated eight hundred kilometres away. It was either that, or forget about further advancement. And the purpose of the move was to help resurrect a new and badly conceived company branch.

The problems the organisation faced were simply insurmountable. I persevered for years but I'd eventually had enough, and I resigned. The branch folded shortly afterwards. My resignation came after twenty-five years of loyalty that no one could dispute. The year was 1976, and I received nothing from the company - just my own superannuation contribution. Because of this, I vowed that I would never work for another big organisation.

With first and second mortgages, my reluctant wife and I bought businesses, and we became shopkeepers. It seemed that I was determined to spend most of my life, working long hours. However, the decision proved a good one. In four years, we had progressed towards righting the financial wrong that had been done to us.

With heat and humidity, summertime can be the time of plague. I contracted cancer, but was lucky enough to survive. The pestilence continued with a serious heart attack. We were holidaying fifteen hundred kilometres from home. One night, around midnight, I faced a dilemma. Was it severe indigestion that I was suffering, or something worse? In the hospital's emergency section, my systolic blood pressure reached three hundred and fifty over some ridiculously high diastolic figure. Some who believed in predestination suggested that my time was not yet up. Back home, while I was in this far distant hospital facing a life-changing personal drama, our business was being robbed of thousands of dollars.

Depressing as some of this may sound, my wife and I have never been through a valley without looking about us, and identifying those who really deserve pity. We accepted that our lot had always been more positive than negative.

When I was seventy-two, I retired absolutely.

Did facing the autumn of my life faze me? On the contrary, I was ready for it. Neither my future prospects, nor my expectations, were high. I had inherited my father's gammy knees and my mother's enlarged heart. My dad suffered pain for years, and my mum died at just seventy. I was already on borrowed time.

Autumn

Deciduous leaves; blushing, yellowing, browning; falling, dry and shrivelled; wind-swept against walls and fences, into drains and hollows, raked, composted, rained upon; refuge for worms, decomposing, completing the circle of dust to dust. Some, to ashes.

Harvest time; golden grain, ripened fruit, fattened cattle; glorious, breathless days. The gathering in, the sharing, the putting down for the lean times; the freezing, the bottling, the drying; squirreling away for winter survival, fattening up for the big sleep.

I'd worked almost incessantly since before I had turned fourteen – but mostly in situations I thoroughly enjoyed. I'd been in the health food industry for over twenty years, and after having my first heart attack at sixty-nine, the prospect of dying around seventy filled me more with embarrassment than regret.

I was truly about to face the autumn of my life. It was time to start shedding our belongings. But which ones? Firstly, we would downsize. Did we really need a family home, or could we be happy in a unit? I'd read of the early experiences of those who pioneered community living. Units were costed with the help of actuaries, but the bottom lines of the retirement village profit and loss accounts were showing red, and the investors grew anxious. The life expectancy forecast of the prospective residents was made according to existing standards, but the residents were outliving those expectations. So, it was back to the drawing board for the entrepreneurs, and into a village for us. It was stage one of the shedding of our leaves.

Eighteen years later, we are still getting rid of stuff we couldn't part with in our first attempt at downsizing. Valuable English tea and dinner sets, heirlooms of a sort that we had been so proud to own, became part of the jetsam. Books, that we once prized for the knowledge and pleasure they gave us, were boxed for book sales. Some were doomed to be bagged as throw-outs for a dollar a shopping bag full, some even pulped as being worthless. Tools and gadgets that we'd budgeted to buy, were now outdated, and were dumped in the council clean-up.

And where will the smart, three piece navy blue suit that has been hanging in my wardrobe end up? It has been there for thirty years, awaiting the time when it will fit me again. Where else but at the Op-shop, and thence to some young blade who will pay a couple of dollars for it, wear it once for a dress-up party, and then use it to mop up oil spills from the floor of his garage where the sump of his bomb has developed a leak?

I cling to a collection of old-fashioned flat irons. As part of their daily grind, wives and maids in previous centuries would have two or three of these heating on the tops of wood-fired stoves, and, over long hours, be lifting them to and fro, to do their ironing. Following our departures from life, I visualise these relics being tossed as junk into the skip that will be commissioned to get rid of what remains of our treasures.

Much of the harvest we've reaped is still stored on our waistlines. We failed to sweat off, or compensate for, as we promised ourselves we would, the servings of ice cream, chocolate, wine and the like, the removal of which from our diet would have diminished some of life's sparkle.

Were we joining the company of bears, bats, snakes and others who fatten in readiness for the next stage of life?

Winter

In Australia, most of us have no perception of what it is like to endure short days and long nights, together with extreme cold and impenetrable fogs. I for one, wonder how those who live where winter snow and ice are the norm, cope. In that situation, yearning for the comfort that

I have been used to, I believe that I would shift homes and emigrate, if necessary.

Rhetorically, would members of the lower species, like the grasshopper, feel cheated, because their life is no more than a single season? Or would they, like us, rationalise that they are fortunate, because there are others such as the may-fly, whose adult life may be brought to an end within a mere twenty-four hours?

In the animal, reptile or insect kingdom, some remove themselves from the concerns of the living. Their heart rate slows, their body temperature drops until it is almost equal to the freezing climatic temperature, and they retire to a state beyond sleep, to enter true hibernation in which they are virtually dead.

The dead of the winter of our human existence can be likened to permanent hibernation. If the end is not dramatic or accidental, perhaps in loneliness or in pain, we will eventually become weary of life, reach a state of boredom, or lose the will to survive. Gradually we may remove ourselves from the duties and pleasures of everyday life, become satisfied to find a nook where we can rest continually, and perhaps indulge in nostalgic reminiscences, until the day comes when we will fail to respond. No one knows, but many have theories about a transition into another sphere. It would be nice, but there, would you be as you are, and I be as I am? Would we, as many suspect, reincarnate as another who is just entering or re-entering life, or even become a lowlier creature, the fate of bad karma? Or might we, indeed, come face to face with our Maker and, if so, have the opportunity of discussion on the meaning of life, and of why this was so, or why that needed to come to pass?

Me? As my dead of winter approaches, in my present state of mind, I hope to keep snuggling down, and drop off each night, appreciating the blessings that have been mine, as I learnt to do as a child. The circumstances of my passing will be as random as the fortunes of my birth. Socrates suggested that, 'death may be the greatest of all blessings', but, for this to be so, the events leading up to it would be dire. When my time does come, how pleasant it would be to simply fail to wake, and, to quote Socrates' wisdom, 'to enter the longest and most untroubled of all sleeps', free of the night's spoilers like burning feet, jumping legs, cramps, traumatic or embarrassing memories and shocking nightmares.

Few pleasures exceed that of a long and carefree sleep, but, if there is more beyond, that will be an unexpected reward.

Scents of Summer

Mary J O'Rourke

Warm sunny days always evoke the most vivid memories of my childhood, the smells of Summer, of hot Summers so long ago, pleasant smells and unpleasant ones are all there in my mind. We were accustomed to living and playing in what we would now term an unhealthy environment.

Most families in those early wartime days lived in two up, two down houses with just the one cold-water tap, gas lights, bare flag floors and a smelly, long drop lavatory in the yard at the back. There was very little money coming in, but we didn't know any different, so us kids enjoyed ourselves just the same.

Summers usually started in April then. The weather was always fine and sunny and we played down by the River Stink on Nelson Square for hours on end. To us kids it was paradise and we had some happy times there playing on the banks amongst the orange, yellow and brown stones that were dyed these colours by years of pollution from local factories and print works that emptied their waste into the river. Oh how it smelled, but we weren't bothered. There were no fish in that river, just rats, because a lot of the river ran underground.

Buttercups, daisies, clover and dandelions grew in lush abundance along the banks of the river. These were lovingly picked and presented to our Mum in a milk bottle or jam jar and placed on the windowsill. We had walks down the Dunkenhalgh as far as Bluebell Wood for picnics and we would take a bottle of water and jam butties and eat them, sitting among the bluebells in the shaded woods.

On the way back we would pass by the smelly filter beds where human waste was processed and then stored in huge square beds. In Summer, these beds dried out and became so hard you could walk across them. We marvelled at the tomato plants that grew alongside these filter beds.

As we made our way up to the swing bridge that spanned the canal, we would wander off the track to go and peer down into the dark depths of a disused and flooded pit air shaft, and drop stones into the bowels of the earth; exciting stuff for us. Everything was an adventure, and we didn't come to any harm.

The swing bridge was good fun: opening and closing it to let the imaginary canal barges through on their way to Leeds or Liverpool, places we had only heard about at school. A scavenge on the Aspen Valley tip would be next, where we sometimes found treasures: buttons, coloured glass and shiny odd shaped pebbles filled our pockets to be played with when we got home.

We would trudge on to the Tar Distilleries. Now that was a beautiful smell, a healthy smell, a clean sharp smell, but mixed with the distinctive aroma of sulphur that always hung in the air over Church Kirk from the Blythes Chemical works, and also the nauseating stench of the bone works on Bridge Street, like rotten cheese.

Continuing along to the Coach Road and Foxhill Bank, we caught butterflies and ladybirds, jumping over the cowpats, playing in the brook and resting a while in the long grass.

The next stop would be the Church and Oswaldtwistle railway station where the kind stationmaster would allow us to sit a while to watch the steam trains pass through on their way to places we had never visited. Ours was such a small world.

The steam trains had a smell that reminded me of the black pea and hot potato stands on the fairground. I remember popping gas tar bubbles between the cobblestones with my fingers on the way home, all squishy and warm, and blackberry picking in late summer.

Playing around the gravestones in the Church cemetery, and the nearby Gatty Park was always great fun on warm summer evenings. Our fun and pleasures were simple and cheap, our imagination was endless, and we never came to any harm. If only life was so carefree for our children now.

Summer Sonnet

Peter Jones

Brown bales of hay dotted in fields of green
Some lovers lazing in the summer sun.
The trees, resplendent, illustrate the scene;
And farmers work until the day is done.
The sheep and cows all settle in repose:
Their tender lambs and calves all snuggle too.
And new-mown hay is heaven to the nose;
The perfect sky, untainted azure blue.
On days like these be thankful you're alive:
This feast of beauty God has made for you.
And those of you who on complaining thrive:
Take time off and appreciate it too.
Our life on Earth is for so short a while:
We mustn't miss a single chance to smile.

Trevor and Tippy's Summer Holiday

Amani Gunawardana

'Come on Trevor, don't be scared!' shouted his sister, Leah. 'The water is warm, just dip your feet in.' Trevor shook his head, 'No thank you, I'll stay here,' he answered. Trevor liked going to the beach, as long as he stayed along the shoreline.

During summer, Trevor's family decided to holiday near the seaside. While Mum and Leah packed their snorkelling gear, Trevor packed his plastic bucket and spade. He also took his favourite teddy, Tippy.

Leah helped Trevor load his suitcase into the boot.

'I can't wait to snorkel,' said Leah, rubbing sun cream around her face.

'I can't wait to build a great big sandcastle with Tippy,' said Trevor, sitting Tippy on his lap.

'I can't wait to relax,' smiled Mum.

Mum reversed the car out of the garage and drove onto the main road. Trevor and Leah put their windows down to let the cool air brush against their faces. Trevor held Tippy close to the window, so he could feel the breeze against his fur too.

It was mid-afternoon when Trevor's family arrived at the caravan park. After unpacking their belongings, they walked down to the beach. On the way, Trevor collected seashells.

'Did you see that tiny crab?' Leah squealed.

'I think we scared it away,' whispered Trevor, 'It disappeared into the sand.'

After Trevor had collected a handful of seashells, Leah and mum decided to go snorkelling.

'Trevor, we'll snorkel in shallow water,' said mum taking a pair of flippers out of her bag. 'Are you sure, you won't come into the water with us?'

Trevor smiled, 'No thank you mum. Tippy and I want to make a sandcastle instead.'

Trevor placed Tippy inside his bucket.

Trevor squinted as Leah and his mother snorkelled in the water, their masks helping them to stay underwater for a long time. Trevor filled his bucket with wet sand as Tippy watched. 'We can decorate our sandcastle with the shells I found,' Trevor said to Tippy, who was covered in sand.

Trevor emptied his bucket onto the sand and used his hands to pat around the edge of the mound. He used his fingers to poke holes into the sand, to make small windows.

Trevor was so busy that he didn't notice the tide brushing against his feet.

'Tippy, you can help me decorate the castle now,' said Trevor turning around to face Tippy.

Swoosh! A wave of water gushed from the sea and took Tippy!

'Tippy! Tippy!' shouted Trevor. He ran along the beach, waving to get Leah and mother's attention.

However, all he could see was their masks bobbing above the water.

Trevor bit his lip, he put one foot into the sea, and then the other. The water tickled his toes. Trevor moved quickly, his fists clenched tightly. Soon the water was knee length deep. Trevor lunged into a wave and pulled Tippy to safety. Mother and Leah, seeing his heroic act, swam back to shore.

'Are you alright?' said Mother, hugging Trevor.

Trevor nodded.

'You went into the water and saved Tippy!' panted Leah.

Trevor held Tippy tightly; his fur was wet and matted.

'Now that you're wet, why don't you snorkel with us?' hinted Leah.

Trevor smiled, 'I might just dip my feet in.'

Mother hugged Trevor for a second time, 'Well, it's a great start,' she laughed.

Trevor watched as mother and Leah continued snorkelling. Holding Tippy tightly, Trevor dipped his feet into the cool sea. The water tickled his toes.

Summer Splendour

Gillian Jones

There is something glorious when you gaze upon an unspoilt meadow on a warm, balmy summer's day.

A taste of what is to come is when you amble by a hedgerow; there the tall cow parsley grows with its white lace-like flowers. Alongside the cow parsley, you will see the common toadflax with yellow, orange, pink or purple flowers that resemble the snapdragons that grow in our gardens. In abundance amongst these flowers grows the stinging nettle, maybe not much fun to the bare flesh of us humans, but a haven for the butterfly larvae. And let's not forget another plant that is not good for us because it's poisonous, but magnificent anyway - the foxglove: a tall bright plant with its distinctive pink bell shaped flowers.

The common daisy with its rosettes of bright green leaves and stems of pretty white flowers, not only adorns our lawns and parks, but grows in abundance in the hedgerows, and alongside the daisy grows the meadow buttercup with its distinctive small bright yellow flowers. Who hasn't spent many hours as a child making buttercup and daisy chains, or putting a buttercup flower under someone's chin to see who likes butter? Also to be found in the hedgerow is the Welsh poppy, not exclusive to Wales; it has dainty attractive yellow petals.

To see an unspoilt meadow is to behold a wondrous arrangement of colour and movement, so it's no wonder many artists have been inspired by loveliness of nature.

There are the dog daisies, tall with dark, vibrant green leaves and large white petals. In contrast to the white flower heads of the daisy, you see the delicate blue petals of the cornflower and its fine feather-like leaves. Majestic is a word that describes the corn marigold, its yellow daisy-like petals are so vibrant. Diversely there is the field forget-me-not with its tiny fragile multiple pale pink or blue flower heads.

Another tall white plant that you will find in a meadow is the corn chamomile, also with its daisy-like flowers and green fern-like foliage. And who could fail to fall in love or be moved by a meadow, bountiful with the corn poppy, large and showy, with vivid red petals and at its centre a black spot; sensational.

With its pale purple flowers, hairy stem and leaves, the cotton thistle - also known as the Scotch thistle - is a common plant in the meadow and hedgerows. Amongst the beauty of the plants and their colours are the elegant meadow grasses with their sturdy stalks and long pointed leaves, swaying with the gentle summer breeze.

The wonderful meadow also delights with the sound of the bumblebees busy feeding on nectar and gathering pollen. Meadow grasshoppers and bush-crickets making their chirping signals to each other, goldfinches taking the opportunity to feed off the seeds of the thistles, and the skylark can be heard, its song radiating through the air. Then there are the many species of butterflies that love the meadow flowers, at times in a frenzy flitting from one plant to another.

Whenever you gaze upon a meadow in summer, spend a while soaking in the sights and sounds, because the best thing about it, is that it's...FREE!

Sound Bites

Carol Cooper

Sound Bites
Sicilian sun washing our backs,
Etna smoking and growling threats,
The sea and the sand are Jack's,
To play with.
The sea is ours and the sand,
The fiestas and the tinny band,
Then another growl, another threat,
The holiday is over.
Shall we come back?
To be with Jack?

Wind Dancing
Seagulls are wind dancing.
Some are cheeky:
Snatch food out of your hand,
Greedy young to feed.
Screechy gulls prey on the generous, the gullible,
Who watch them scoop up their squashed pie,
Then shrug their shoulders and make do with chips.
It's a touch of the real world,
Rock hard as the cliffs and the sea.
Yet the gulls are wind dancing;
Wonderful, wonderful wind dancing.

Uncle Utu's Seasonal Umbrella

Amani Gunawardana

Uncle Utu took his umbrella everywhere he went.

He used it during rainy days. He carried it around on sunny days, and even on really windy days.

I asked Uncle Utu why he needed an umbrella, but he just smiled and said that it always came in handy.

For example, he used his umbrella as a sword, when playing the Castle Knight at the local theatre.

During spring, he used it to ward off magpies, when walking home from the shopping centre.

And last summer, he even used it to signal the lifeguards, during his trip to the beach.

Once in a while, Uncle Utu used his umbrella as most people do.

The residents in his neighbourhood thought he was strange. He would often be seen walking down the street with an open umbrella.

'He doesn't want to mess up his hairstyle,' said Mrs Winters.

'He thinks his umbrella makes him invisible,' said Mr Horace.

'No, he's just peculiar,' said Mrs Roberts.

Uncle Utu was used to such comments, so he made sure to hum loudly as he walked past each house.

One day Uncle Utu lost his companion.

He spent the whole day searching the house in a frantic state, but couldn't find it anywhere.

From that day on, Uncle Utu locked himself in his room.

I bought him a new umbrella, but he preferred the old one.

Mum bought a similar model from the internet, but he groaned and complained that it wasn't the same.

Grandma even searched through every umbrella store in the land, but no one stocked Uncle Utu's favourite umbrella.

I decided to find Uncle Utu's umbrella.

First, I searched the house. Then I searched the garage. Finally, I visited all the places he did, but I didn't have any luck.

'Uncle Utu, why was your umbrella so important?' I asked.

'It was one of a kind,' he answered.

'What do you mean?' I inquired. 'What made it so special?'

'Firstly, it was reversible. It had blue and yellow polka dots on one side and white and grey stripes on the other. And secondly, it had a small pocket near the handle, so I could hide my secret business,' he whispered.

'Secret business?' I exclaimed.

Uncle Utu covered my mouth.

'I will not speak any more of it,' he hissed and ushered me out of his room.

Two Continents

I spent the whole day wondering what Uncle Utu meant by his secret business, but either way, I was determined to help him.

I searched the internet once again, until my eyes came across a flyer which was going to solve Uncle Utu's problem.

The next day I showed Uncle Utu my leaflet. He leaped out of bed, grabbed his baseball cap and sprinted out the door.

That evening, my Uncle came home with a brand new umbrella, exactly like the old one. It had blue and yellow polka dots on one side and white and grey stripes on the other. It also had a small pocket near the handle, so he could keep his secret business.

'Yippee! The umbrella making class was a success,' I cheered.

Uncle Utu nodded, 'Once again, I have my very own custom made umbrella.'

Uncle Utu yanked off his cap -and then it happened.

I witnessed first-hand, what my uncle was trying to hide all along…

His toupee slipped off his head and fell to the floor!

Uncle Utu took a small glue stick out of his top drawer and fixed his hair. Then he carefully placed the tube of glue into the small pocket in his umbrella.

My heart skipped a beat, as I looked up at my uncle's face.

'You're secret's safe with me,' I whispered.

Uncle Utu sat on his bed and let out a big sigh!

'See how my umbrella always comes in handy?' said Uncle Utu, with a twinkle in his eye.

Summer Story

Peter Jones

As a lifelong lover of the city of my father's birth, I have visited Edinburgh on many occasions. One regret I have, however, is that I have never attended the famous Tattoo. Watching it on television is a poor substitute for what I am assured is a ceremony filled with atmosphere, and is a wonderful spectacle.

I can only cite as my excuse, the fact that when I went as a child, it was always in the Accrington holiday fortnight, which was invariably the third and fourth weeks of July, a couple of weeks before the Edinburgh Festival, of which the Tattoo is the centrepiece, begins. As a result I was always back home by then.

With the exception of one weekend, I have never been in the city at that time and the one time I was, my car broke down and the weekend was spent retrieving it. What I can say is that when we arrived in the city centre that Friday night at around 1.30 a.m. it was absolutely heaving with tourists, very well lit and bursting with life.

As most of our Scottish holidays were at the height of summer, for the most part, we had some wonderful weather. In the summer, Scotland is such a tourists' pleasure. Once you escape the cities, you can drive for miles without seeing another vehicle and the roads are so full of wonderful views, especially when you venture further north and west.

Amongst the gems we have uncovered over the years was Loch Lomond, with the biggest mountain in Britain at its northernmost tip, Ben Nevis, and Fort William at the end of a twenty-two mile boat trip.

Pitlochry, at the gateway to the highlands, is another beauty spot and we were fortunate enough to be there in the scorching summer of 1976.

Scotland is also famous for its castles. Apart from the famous Edinburgh Castle, there is Stirling Castle, the beautiful Eilean Donan Castle, the imposing Glamis Castle and many more. When you think of castles you think of battles. Culloden, Prestonpans, Stirling Bridge and Falkirk come to mind.

Perhaps the bloodiest battles took place in the midst of the imposing hills of Glencoe where two feuding families caused mayhem: the Campbells and the McDonalds. It ended with the massacre of thirty-eight members of Clan McDonald for not pledging allegiance to the newly crowned William and Mary quickly enough, and the subsequent death of forty women and children of the same clan from exposure due to their houses being burned to the ground.

Of course, all that is long in the past and Scotland is one of the most beautiful countries in the world when the sun is shining, and always a pleasure to visit. I do think they have a cheek calling me a Sassenach though, when most of my family is Scottish.

It is two years since I was last in Scotland, but hopefully I will be back there soon. If they do get home rule and independence from Westminster as Alex Salmond is hoping, I wonder if we will then need passports to visit. On the plus side, just think of all that duty free Scotch we can bring home.

My Apple Tree

Doris Sharp

In Spring she stands.
pleasing my sight;
radiantly dressed
in pink and white.
Blossom though, falls,
Still, beauty is seen.
She has changed her clothes
To fresh-leaved green.

Soon, carefully look,
even more she enhances;
tiny fruits have appeared
upon her branches.
Summer's warmth aids
this story's telling –
the fruits are developing,
richly swelling.

Autumn now sees her,
her promise keeping:
rosy apples, ripened
ready for reaping.
Despite the striving
through long night and day
to attain this fulfilment,
all is now stripped away.

Two Continents

Winter renders her
stark and bare,
as though Mother Nature
holds no care.
Magic, the orchestration
of soil, sun and rain,
that will see her play out
this silent symphony
again, again and again.

Autumn

The Nose Knows

Rita Hodgson

It's August.
The calendar says it's still winter,
Still a month before our twelve hour day.
Yet nature is so busy starting up her engines
After a cold wet sleep,
That signs of spring are heavy on the air,
And the wattles are painting the landscape
In swathes of yellow.

Shoots in the garden beds,
A haze of leaves on branches
Buds of pitostrum, prunus, honeysuckle,
Hyacinth, rhodies and roses,
- and the ubiquitous onion weed,
Promising to fill the air with scent and pollen.

Today my nose and I went for a wander.
Poor thing, it is feeling a bit like spring has sprung –
You know – sniffles and sneezes,
Without any sign of a cold.

Everything was burgeoning,
Flowers, shrubs, weeds, all mixed in together,
All busy starting another season,
Another spring, another abundance.
This glorious promise of renaissance lasts

Four Seasons
such a short time.
In a few weeks the bees will be busy,
The fruit will be setting,
And blossoms blowing away.

Each season follows the other,
Paying lip service to our calendar,
While Mother Nature, left to herself
Follows her own piper,
Dancing through cycle after cycle
Of miracles.

Passages of Time

Joan M Crossley

Eva lay sprawling, her body strewn across the bed, her face flushed with concentration and exasperation.

Alongside her was an old photo album, but some of the frail snapshots of black and white images began sliding towards the floor, together with her reading glasses and mobile phone. Angrily pushing her faded curls away from now tired eyes, she tried to focus on the digital clock.

This was to no avail. With a sigh of frustration, she lay prone, her head turned on the soft pillow, almost promptly falling into a welcome dreamy sleep…

* * *

Eva could hear a booming tick-tock, tick-tock sound. It was coming from the railway station clock. Strange - she could hear the sounds despite the scores of people milling around the platform, either waiting to board the oncoming train, or greet their nearest and dearest. The train began hissing and belching steam as it approached the station. The ground vibrated underneath Eva's small feet.

Janet, Eva's mummy, grabbed her hand in excitement exclaiming, "Oh! Eva, isn't it lovely? Your Grandpa James is coming to stay with us - all the way from Scotland!"

"Why? Is it 'cause Granny Mollie went up to heaven?" questioned Eva, looking up into her mummy's lovely dark eyes, observing her mother's auburn curls bobbing up and down.

"Oh yes sweetheart," Janet replied, bending down to hug her daughter, her eyes glistening with unshed tears. "Daddy will be able to learn more about gardening and planting our own fruit and veg. As we used to say, we'll make do and mend Eva".

Eva pondered, wondering what this statement actually meant.

"Daddy works so hard in that factory doesn't he? He gets lots of pennies for us!" Eva had to shout, raising her voice above the continuing noise of the station and the loud ticking sound.

Janet began eagerly urging Eva along the platform.

"Oh! Of course he does Eva, but Grandpa James is an expert gardener. Perhaps he'd enjoy making a small lawn for you to play on, and your baby sister Anna could lie on a rug surrounded by the fresh green grass in the summer eh?"

Eva was considering this obviously important point, and her hand was sweating, because her mummy was clasping it so tightly. Janet bent again and kissed the top of Eva's head, adding anxiously, "I do hope Anna is still asleep after her feed. It was so good of Mrs Henry to offer to mind her for us this afternoon Eva".

* * *

As she tossed and turned in her fitful sleep, the ticking and tocking got louder in Eva's ears, along with bright happy images of her dearest Grandpa, who took her to the park and the wild woodland areas, explaining all about nature, often bending down to study a weed or a flower. She loved it when his moustache tickled her face. Concentrating on the long complicated words, she would often try to repeat them to baby Anna, who chuckled and babbled in her pram, especially when Eva gave her a lick of the ice-cream cone that Grandpa James had bought for her...

The clock suddenly stopped, when Eva was taken into the back room of their cottage.

Grandpa was lain, stiff as a statue, white as marble, his whiskers not moving or tickling her cheek.

"Grandpa-Grandpa! Wake up!" Eva's cries were in vain.

The silence was deafening...

Eva woke up drenched in sweat, crying out, "I could see Grandpa at last! As plain as day Paul! Paul what a strange dream after all these years..." Eva's voice trailed off.

The silence in the room was absolute...

Eva almost fell off the edge of the single bed that had been her mother's in earlier years. Momentarily she'd forgotten that she wasn't at home with her husband. No, she'd offered to stay the night in the cottage, to try and sort through her late mother's possessions, before putting the old cottage on the market.

Hastily grabbing robe and slippers, Eva collected her reading glasses from the floor. A dim light from the moon shone through the old draughty window. What was that skittering outside? Probably a rabbit or squirrel, out for an early morning breakfast...

As she padded along the old passages towards the stairs and the welcome kitchen, she could almost hear her mother calling out, "Do you want a cuppa love?"

'No, I need something stronger mum', she thought, as she tried flicking the light switch, shivering in the dim light, with no warming radiators.

"Oh God mum, why didn't you try to persuade dad to get this place modernized?"

The old walls echoed at the sound of her voice, and the floors creaked and groaned as she made her way down to the kitchen. At least the light was better here.

She glanced at her wristwatch, it was 2am, too late to ring Paul and she'd left her mobile upstairs. She made her way to the kettle.

She spied a bottle of her late father's whiskey in the old cabinet, and muttered, "Must be at least a decade old-what the heck!" and even though she disliked the smell, she downed a small glass and proceeded to wander into the back room where she'd left her laptop. Switching on the old lamp, she surveyed the disarray that she and Anna had caused earlier. Pots, pans, ornaments, clothes, books - all the memorabilia of times past which had caused such a verbal melee between the two sisters.

Stepping over half a dozen cardboard boxes, Eva tenderly touched the old rocking chair in which her parents had often sat; and thought sadly that her grandpa must have enjoyed the padded softness here too. There were slight imprints on the very old faded cushions.

Eva shivered, then thought she heard a blackbird singing in the old oak tree outside the rickety window, "You are an early bird! Of course it was Grandpa who taught me to recognize you..." she whispered to the room now devoid of welcoming voices...

Unnerved by this sudden thought, she realized that her laptop was sitting on the old coffee table. It was still open and plugged into a dubious socket. Hastily putting on her specs' she realized that there was one e-mail. It was from her as-usual blunt-worded sister.

Eva read the script:

Hi sis,

Hells Bells! Your mobile is off! I agree with you! The time isn't right to sell the cottage.

That load of stuff you sent me home with has revealed all sorts! Not least-a plan of the cottage! It has a hidden cellar!! Could it have been used during the 2nd World War, before we were born?

We could somehow get the finances to do the cottage up. Perhaps your Rob might like to rent it, he could have a music room in the cellar, or our Amy could use it for a photographic studio. Don't contact the estate agent yet Eva!!

We need to talk.... Sorry about the row. Luv' you loads... Anna. Xxx

Eva was sure she could hear a very loud ticking noise, and then a clock chiming exultantly....

Chronicles of young Love

Lilian Coffa

Carmen stared at the computer screen for what felt like forever. She had not written a single word since she opened up the new word document. Scratch that...she actually had, she just deleted them. They were the usual words that started a sentence; 'the', 'once', 'at', and the actual name of the leading character, Elizabeth.

Carmen thumped her head against the desk top. She officially had writer's block. Jolly - for no one who gave a damn if she wrote another story or not, but not so for her publisher. She had been on a hiatus for three months, to grieve over her father's death, but now people were breathing down her neck, wanting the next sale.

So Carmen decided on a story that she had come up with years ago. She thought it would have been easy enough, she had the general outline of it in her head. A young and beautiful girl called Elizabeth, drama, drama, then something to do with vampires, maybe a werewolf, a stud for a love interest, a couple of kissing scenes, drama drama, the end.

She pulled her glasses off and rubbed her eyes. *I'm brain dead*, she whined to herself. Raising her head she peered over the laptop at the kitchen on the other side of the room. *Brain food.*

"Protein," she declared to herself as she got out of the chair, thinking of the deli meat in the fridge. She came back with a bag of cookies. After five minutes of surfing

YouTube, Carmen wiped her hands on her jeans and tried again.

Elizabeth...

Delete!

The moon was...

Delete!

Carmen's ears pricked up to the sound of keys and the unlocking of the front door.

"HELLO!" Came a shout.

Carmen cringed. Rebecca was home. She leaned back on her desk chair, craning her neck to look around the corner. Rebecca was in the hallway, sitting on the bottom step of the staircase, taking off her school shoes. She was Carmen's little sister, sixteen, and ten years younger than the writer.

"How was your day?" Carmen asked.

Rebecca raised her head, pulling her long dark hair behind her ear. She had a stupid grin on her face. "Jay likes me."

Carmen paused a moment, a mental list running through her mind. *Which one was Jay again?*

Rebecca noticed the strain in Carmen's eyes. "Jay. Plays football. A senior."

"Right! Jay," cried Carmen. "Jay the jock."

"Yeah, anyway, today after class, he told me he liked me," Rebecca gushed, before squealing in delight.

Carmen feigned excitement. "*Yay*."

"I know, right! We exchanged numbers...do you think he'll call today? He has to call today."

At that point, Carmen returned to her computer. "I'm sure he'll call," she muttered, suddenly exhausted by her sister's antics.

Rebecca glided into the office, as if walking on air. "He's so hot," she continued, grabbing Carmen's bag of cookies and settling into the bean bag in the corner.

A vague mental image of Jay flashed in Carmen's mind. She remembered him at the last football game. Tall, blonde, muscular, he seemed to tick all the boxes.

"It's like Romeo and Juliet," sighed the teenager, rummaging her hand around for a choc chip.

Carmen's eyes slid to her sister. "You do know how that ends, right?"

Rebecca pouted. "I didn't mean literally," she snapped before throwing a pillow at her sister. She had finally caught onto Carmen's sarcasm. "How would you know what love is anyway? You write fantasy, not romance. And you haven't had a date in over a year."

"Ouch," Carmen winced, *kitty cat's got her claws out today*. "Okay, number one, every single one of my stories has a romantic subgenre and number two," she paused. "Give me a minute."

"HA!" cried Rebecca, pointing her finger at her sister. "See, you can't judge!"

Carmen rolled her eyes and snatched the bag of cookies from her sister's grip. "Alright! You made your point. Now go be lovey dovey somewhere else. I have work to do."

"Fine," huffed Rebecca, rolling off the bean bag and sashaying into the kitchen. "You're just jealous."

"Oh believe me," bit Carmen, swerving around to her computer again. "I'm not jealous of Jay the jock."

Rebecca poked her head around the corner. "Why can't you just be happy for me? First love, flowers, springtime..."

Carmen stopped chewing on her cookie. *Springtime...*

"What?" demanded Rebecca, noticing the spaced out look on her sister's face.

"Nothing," mumbled Carmen, chewing furiously. She hastily wiped the crumbs from her mouth before placing her fingers on the keys again.

It was a fine spring morning the day that Elizabeth first laid eyes on...Joseph...

Spring

Carmen sat at her desk typing away furiously at her laptop. It had been a week and a half since Rebecca and Jay hooked up, and Carmen suddenly found herself with so much material to work with. Every day when her sister came home from school, she would ask her how her day was and all she ever heard about was Jay, Jay, and Jay. Her story was flowing out of her like a volcano. Elizabeth was an eighteen year old girl heading off to college. There she meets a boy called Joseph, who people steered clear of. There was just something about him that felt ancient. The question was... vampire or werewolf? She envisioned Joseph to be tall, dark and handsome, with piercing blue eyes that stared at Elizabeth with no inhibitions. *Why was he so interested in her?*

Carmen eyed her sister one night, as Rebecca sat on the couch with a bowl of M&Ms watching *Keeping up with the Kardashians*.

"Becky," she started, and then waited for the glare that she knew her sister would throw at her. It came.

"What?" whined Rebecca. She didn't like being interrupted while she was watching her favourite show.

"Has Jay ever told you what he likes best about you?" she asked. She watched her sister's eyes light up at the sound on Jay's name. Carmen felt like gagging.

"He said the first thing he liked about me was my smile."

Carmen bit her lip, it wasn't good enough, too cliché. How about...

"Why are you staring at me?" demanded Elizabeth, scowling at Joseph, as he leaned against her locker. He gave her a lopsided smile. "I like your tattoo."

Much better, thought Carmen as she continued typing away. Her publisher called the next day, and she was happy to report that the story was coming along well.

Then her joy was short lived when the man delivered her a deadline. Carmen hated deadlines.

Another week passed. Carmen sat cross legged on her bed, nursing a cold that she had been given by her ever generous cousin Alex. A cup of Lipton tea sat on her side table as she hunched over her computer, a pile of tissues becoming a mountain at the end of her bed. She had spent the day being lazy, watching TV and grazing. By four in the afternoon, she started to feel guilty that she hadn't written anything for the last two days, so she had opened her computer and began.

But her momentum only lasted twenty minutes when she suddenly became aware of a presence at the doorway. She jolted at the sight of her sister. The girl was still in her school uniform. "GOD Becky!" exclaimed Carmen, holding her chest. "You scared the shit out of me. When did you get home? I didn't hear you come in."

Rebecca didn't answer. She had a weird look on her face, something between guilt and satisfaction. Her cheeks were flushed, but she didn't look sick.

Carmen narrowed her eyes. "What happened?"

Rebecca focused on the mountain of tissues as she answered.

"We did it."

Carmen's eyes grew wide. *We did it? As in...IT?* She closed her laptop slowly.

"Was this your first time?"

Rebecca nodded shyly. Carmen's throat felt thick as she swallowed. "Are you OK?"

A small smile crept on her sister's lips. "It was perfect."

A mental image of the deed flashed in Carmen's mind. Then she made the mistake of sticking her sister's head on the headless female doing the act. Suddenly her stomach churned. *Block it out*, she yelled to herself. *Block it out!*

Taking Carmen's silence as a good sign, Rebecca came into the room and sat on the edge of the bed. A few tissues fell to the ground. "It hurt a little bit, at the beginning, but after that it was really good. He knew what he was doing."

A look of horror crossed Carmen's face. "Do I look like I want details?"

The colour in her face, which had just started coming back, suddenly vanished. She felt a relapse coming on.

"I've never seen a...well it before....and to tell you the truth, it sort of grossed me out in the beginning."

Carmen put her hands on her ears. "Urgh! Too much information. I don't want to know, I don't want to know," she wailed.

Rebecca glared at her sister. "What the hell is wrong with you? I'm trying to confide and you're being rude."

"I don't want details Becky."

The concept that Rebecca was no longer a virgin irked her. In Carmen's eyes she was still just ten years old, still a baby.

"You're such a bitch," huffed Rebecca and she charged out of the room.

"And you shouldn't be having sex until you're thirty," Carmen called out.

Rebecca's answer came from the bathroom. "What? Like you?"

Carmen grimaced. "Whatever," she mumbled, opening her lap top again and titling a new word document. The blossomed flower...*block it out, block it out*!!!

Summer

Ten days later Carmen was seriously considering scrapping the project. Using her sister as a muse had just taken a turn for the uncomfortable. What had started out as young love between Rebecca and her jock had turned into a saga of heated passion. They were at it like rabbits, every day according to the loved up teenager. It was becoming too much for Carmen. She couldn't look at her sister without plastering her head on Elizabeth's body. She should have picked someone else.

Carmen sat on the toilet seat, severely constipated after a week of having take-out every night. She never fared well with noodles. The pile of magazines in the corner of the little room lay untouched, out of date and skimmed through a hundred times. It lay as a pedestal for the last roll of toilet paper in the house.

Carmen made a mental note to write it down on the white board in the kitchen.

Suddenly a sharp knock came at the door. Carmen stilled, dread spreading through her.

"Carmen?" her sister started.

"Yes?" she replied, cringing, her voice sounded guilty.

"Do you have my iPad in there?"

Busted. "Maybe."

Rebecca sighed with exasperation. "How many times have I asked you not to take it in the toilet?!"

Later on that day Carmen sat at her desk, drumming her fingers along the polished wood of the table top.

"Give it back!" demanded Elizabeth, reaching up for her iPad. Joseph had it in his hand, held high up above his head, out of her reach. The smug look on his face was irritating her.

"Say please," he said, his eyes twinkling with mischief. Elizabeth huffed. "Please!"

"Say it nicely," he added, now hiding the iPad behind his back. Elizabeth narrowed her eyes and lunged forward, trying to reach around him. His free hand caught her wrist and held her in place. Her face was an inch from his, she could smell the mint on his breath. He popped breath mints like they were pills. A sudden churning in her belly erupted. There was hunger in his eyes...

Autumn

Three more weeks of nauseating puppy love passed. Carmen was starting to cringe now whenever Rebecca talked about Jay. There was nothing new, nothing to further along the story. Then just when she thought about diverting her attention from Rebecca, her sister came home one day sulking.

Carmen swirled around in her chair, innately attuned to her sister's mood. She tried to feign ignorance.

"Everything okay?" she asked sweetly as Rebecca sank down into the bean bag.

"Jay is such an asshole," seethed Rebecca.

The corner of Carmen's mouth twitched. *Finally...*

"What happened?"

"Nothing. But I don't like the attitude he's been giving me. He told me to shut up today! In front of his friends! He made me look like an idiot. I was just asking if he could drive me to the Retirement Home so I could do my volunteering today. I had to ask Samantha's brother instead."

Carmen opened her mouth to say something nice, but her sister suddenly jumped up from the bean bag. "Where's the iPod? I need some music therapy."

"It's in the breadbox," replied Carmen, her eyes following Rebecca as she marched into the kitchen. *Jay had better be careful*, she thought, *he wouldn't like to meet Becky the bitch.* As soon as the young girl was out of sight, Carmen returned to her computer and rummaged around the drawers for her memory stick.

"How dare you tell me to shut up!" hissed Elizabeth. She was struggling to keep up with Joseph as he strode across the long corridor.

"It wasn't your place to answer back," his voice was clipped. "You do not disrespect the Count. Now we have to deal with the repercussions."

Winter

Three days later Carmen jolted at the sound of the front door slamming loudly with excessive force.

"THE BASTARD!!!" yelled Rebecca.

Carmen jumped out of the seat and flew to the entrance. "What happened!" she demanded wildly, her eyes roaming up and down her sister, assessing any physical injuries. Her eyes finally rested on her sister's eyes, they were red and glistening with angry tears.

Rebecca made a gurgling noise, then fell into Carmen's un-awaiting arms. The writer barely had a second to brace for the sudden weight on her. Gently she patted the teenagers back. "Shhh," she soothed.

The girl sniffed loudly and Carmen stiffened. "If you dare wipe your nose on this shirt you're cleaning it yourself."

Carmen got a muffled reply and a defiant shrug. She sighed and dragged her sister up the stairs to her bedroom. "Now tell me what happened," she said, seating the girl on her bed. She started removing Rebecca's garments one by one. First one shoe, then the other, then the jacket and the half-eaten packet of M&Ms hidden deep in one pocket. *I thought she was on a new diet?*

She handed Rebecca a box of tissues and sat down next to her, tucking the girl's hair behind her ear. Carmen's temper flared slightly at the sight of her sister in derail. *That bum did this to her,* she thought angrily. She waited for Rebecca to speak.

Through quivering lips, the young girl told her how the day had started out so normal. "It was just fine this morning. We went to our classes, made plans to meet up at lunch. When class finished, I had to go to the toilet. While I was in there I heard these girls come in. I don't know who they were but I've seen them around enough. And I heard them talk about Jay, how he was screwing one of their friends. And I was thinking to myself, *but I don't know these girls*, then I realized how stupid I was."

Carmen nodded in sympathy. "He was cheating on you."

Rebecca sniffed. "I confronted him about it, and he denied it at first, but I could see it in his eyes."

"Oh Becky," sighed Carmen, rubbing her sister's arm affectionately. "If a person hurts you this much then they are not worth it. You'll find another guy who'll treat you better."

"But I loved him," she choked, turning her head into the crook of her sister's arm. Carmen seriously doubted it, she was too young to know what real love was. Teenagers were always so dramatic. Still, this had to be some kind of record, four seasons in two months!

"Just forget about him Becky, he's a year older than you so you won't have to see him, you have different classes."

Rebecca raised her head up, the look on her face sent shivers down Carmen's spine. She had her father's eyes, the Sicilian look. "He's not getting off that easy. He's going to pay."

The next day Carmen noticed a new song had been added to the iPod, *Titanium*, Rebecca's idea of a pick-me-up. Then at around lunch time, while she was deliberating between chicken salad and souvlaki the phone rang. It was the principal of Rebecca's school, informing her that her little sister had just run over Jay's foot with his own car, crippling him, just three days before the big game.

So, Carmen thought, placing the phone down after the conversation ended, *the Sicilian has awakened*. Scrambling around the house, she collected her wallet, phone and car keys before rushing out the door. *And they used to say I was the wayward child!*

The house lay quiet on her exit, except for the humming of the laptop she had forgotten to shut down, and the word document she had left open.

How could I have trusted him, Elizabeth thought bitterly, angry at her own naivety of the situation. She had fancied herself in love, and now she had a new pair of fangs to show for it. Joseph had made her a vampire against her own will. This was not what she wanted, not death. Elizabeth stared out of the window, watching the colours of the night turn lighter as dawn approached. She would have to close the curtains soon. Her gaze turned dark as her resolve hardened. He will pay, she thought vengefully, and it would be his own fault for turning a Sicilian into a vampire...

Autumn Evening

Rita Hodgson

All day the leaves have fallen
Drifting, swirling, dancing
Down to the forest floor
Warm hues of autumn,
Golden light on golden leaves

Now, clouds collect on the horizon,
Gossiping birds circle,
And nature holds its breath,
Waiting for the sun to set.

The organ thunders, choirs join in.
Alleluia!
Look! Look at the sky!
Great golden sculptures made of fire,
Moving, changing,
Each vista more amazing than the last.

Slowly the sun sinks
The miracle continues – colours are muted now,
And in the gloaming the lone piper plays.

When the show ends,
'Author, Author' we cry into the darkness.
'Encore, Encore!'

On cue, the moon comes up.

Autumn in New England

Linda Ann Ford

The air turns sharply brisk
and whispers the scent of leaves
drying in the autumn sun.
Dried-out corn stalks,
kissed by an early frost,
rallied together in their final hour as decoration.
Trees put on their bright arrays
and dance to the rhythm of the wind
which threatens their hold on life.
Roadside stands turn shades of orange,
as the gathered pumpkins call out
for chance of another life as a jack-o-lantern.
The children, in moments of pause,
stop to pet a newborn calf, focusing on the softness
and the wonder of this miracle of life.
Vendors serve up pumpkin soup and apple cobbler...
tastes of the season
to tickle the palates and warm the soul.
Festivals to celebrate the harvest
echo through the hills of New England,
bringing song to the earth, as it readies for winter's sleep.

An Autumn Tale

David Berry

It had been a blisteringly hot summer. Unbelievable temperatures and water shortages never experienced before on such a scale. In fact, horror of all horrors: water rationing in England. How can this be?

Villages long since lost to secure our supplies for the future reappeared in reservoirs. Early cottages, a church and a bridge came from their watery grave. Oh how fragile our supplies really are.

Cities like Manchester actually pumped water from the Lake District, some ninety miles away to quench the thirst of their citizens, but the not-so-lucky residents of Harrogate had to queue at mobile water tankers; very large articulated trucks to get their share of the merged supply.

But now, the aftermath of this: Mother Nature creates massive destructive thunderstorms and floods, yes floods, so powerful that houses collapse, bridges are swept away, businesses destroyed in seconds, crops decimated and cows and sheep left stranded on small islands created by the raging floods. Treasured possessions from flooded homes are lost and scattered to the four winds, uprooted trees which had stood proud for eighty, ninety years now reduced to matchwood, kindling for the middle class' wood burning stoves in their country retreats.

Farmers, landowners and families try to come to terms with these devastating losses for all of them, yet more suffering is heaped onto a struggling populous with food shortages, higher prices and no hope of escape. Welcome to Autumn.

Time to reflect on this colourful and normally beautiful time of year. Deciduous trees having seen that winter is just around the corner, creating colourful leaf displays that take your breath away, squirrels busily gathering all the forest's plentiful bounty and secreting it for the winter they've yet to face. But that's not the only battle these little red creatures have to encounter.

Along came the grey squirrel: more powerful, more aggressive. And the greys systematically decimated the reds to small areas in the north of England, Scotland, small areas of Wales, and very small pockets in the south of England. Not only were the reds physically massacred by the greys, they also introduced the squirrel box virus. But now the greys face their own nemesis: the super greys; nature's way of moving on I suppose. Survival of the fittest, as we say.

Onto the rutting season. Whoever has the biggest antlers wins the ladies. I suppose in some ways this can lead to a role reversal. All the males saying to their prospective mates, "Not today Bambi, I've got a headache."

A new generation to be created, the proud stag surveying his hard won territory, an amazing silhouette on the bracken covered hillside. Shy retiring animals, but sadly no match for the poachers' gun or the laird's culling programme.

Elderberries, blackberries and a multitude of other wild berries ripe and ready to eat; some we can eat and enjoy, only to be enjoyed by birds and animals.

Nature saying we all have our place.

The lovely butterfly gathers nectar from the blackberry blossom then goes on to feast on the cluster of berries he or she helped to create. Badgers love blackberries too. They're more raucous when feasting, acting as nature's pruning machine, which encourages next year's new growth. And so the cycle continues.

Orchards bursting at the seams; tough little trees that have laughed at the storms.

Apples, pears, cherries, gooseberries, strawberries and raspberries long gone, but for all our cider makers - bingo! English fruit for English loony juice. Try some, especially Merrydown.

Then there's the Mothers' Union annual outings at the local agricultural shows; the Jam Brigade. Mrs Cynthia Mountshaft De-veer ('don't forget the hyphen'), normally unbearable, but upstaged this time by a Mrs Audrey Smith with her wonderful three berry surprise. One up for us comers eh!

These agricultural shows in Autumn give our struggling farmers time to let their hair down and show off that prize bull; magnificent, strong, but scary too.

Sheep with strange markings standing out from the crowd and chickens with un-pronounceable names, looking splendid with their pompom heads and weird hairy feet.

Funny misshaped vegetables - we all know the type - bring a smile and a giggle. First prize awarded. Fifteen years of selective breeding, loads of love and care, 'Dad, you would have been proud.' Well done to everyone. You deserve it.

Farm machinery on display that's out of Star Wars, more levers, rotation than the moon, and more gadgets than you could shake a stick at. Wi-Fi, hi-fi, air conditioning, vanity mirror eh! Wonders of technology.

Must admit I'm jealous and envious. Far different from my days of real horse power, but then they're just machines. Susie, my lovely shire, was a real, breathing wonder. Then, a real rarity and gem for me, a shire horse parade, brewers holding onto their heritage drays, so elaborate you have to admire them, and the shires powerful, shiny and majestic. Pinch me, I'm so happy.

But Mother Nature hasn't finished with us yet. All those lovely deciduous trees start to shed their leaves. Carpets of gold, bronze, yellow, brown, red, and some still green, cover the forest floor, urban roads, country lanes, parks, and even our gardens. No-one escapes this spectacle.

Dads hiding their offspring in leaf mounds, waiting for an unsuspecting Mum to pass by. Then, the leaves erupt and son number two sends Mum scuttling away screaming; magical family moments.

Children off to school dragging leaves into accurate piles neatly placed about ten feet apart. Then my favourite bird, the skilful swallow, skims past with Euro-fighter precision as you walk down a country lane. Brunel would have been proud of a swallow nest. Mud, sticks and grass stuck to a wall with an entrance the size of a 50p. How does it stay in place like that? It's also conker season; all those wonderful formulas to have the hardest, toughest, shiniest, brown beauty that could annihilate the opposition with one crack.

Early advice from my Dad: "Soak it in vinegar and let it dry naturally, then oven bake for five and a half minutes in Mum's coal fired oven."

That's fine, but I didn't get any of them past an eighter, that means eight straight wins. My Uncle Gill told me he had a better method. He told me to get a conker about 1 1/4" across, a biggie.

I met my mate Michael McGuire, but we couldn't find any suitable conkers, so we went to the Dunkenhalgh Estate at Clayton-le-Moors. Michael said, "Watch this Dave," and he took a catapult out of his pocket and - wham! Down came this brilliant conker from the horse chestnut tree and off we went to Uncle Gill's.

When we got to his house at Kingsley Close, Uncle Gill said, "That's a good un, watch and learn." He carefully sliced the bottom off the conker then said, "Now for the secret ingredient, liquid quick drying cement."

He holed out the conker and poured the cement into it and then when it was almost set, he pushed a small nail through it for the string to go through, and said, "When it's properly dry, I'll stick the bottom back on and you'll have the Daddy of all conkers."

Guess what? Unbeaten all season.

Now if you want to play conkers at school, you have to wear safety goggles and protective gloves. Next year you'll probably need a helmet too. No fun anymore.

The winds of change are blowing, winter is on its way. The weak won't survive. This autumnal cleansing, trees will lose their leaves recycled as leaf mould, protecting our insect life, and some of the seeds shed from other plants over the winter. Unpicked fruit becomes more compost. Some animals won't make it again.

Culling the weak – nature's way, but autumn does have its own beauty and its place in our seasons. Spring the renewal, summer the bloom, autumn the cleanse, and the winter yet to come. Nature's greatest challenge for us, our animal neighbours, and all the countryside fauna and flora.

Autumn Morning

Rita Hodgson

Before dawn, and it's misty, so misty and still
There are no colours, only shades of grey
Even sound has lost its way.

Breathe in, breathe out.

In the small light the hills are haloed,
Their contours softened, their distances defined,
Their feet buried in grey,
In oceans of grey cloud.

Breathe in, breathe out.

Yesterday we raked leaves, collected fallen bark.
Lit a fire, and watched the smoke rise up,
Up into the still moist air.
Today the world is scented with incense.

Breathe in, breathe out.

Dawn and a gentle morning breeze
Add colour and movement.
And as the sun comes up
It changes pastels to
The glorious colours of Exotic Fall
Bright leaves, ripe apples, pumpkins

125

Four Seasons
Still decorated with skeins of mist.

Breathe in, breathe out.

Background music swells
A flute solo, then reveille
Into a fanfare of trumpets.

What a sensuous experience!
Oh! What a morning!

Breathe in, breathe out.

Changing Seasons

Linda Ann Ford

Still and crisp, the air has changed.
Soon the seasons re-arrange.
Stretch out for warmth, the summer blooms,
with daydreams of the days in June.
When all the earth, with blankets green,
all varying hues of colors seen.
Each tree with heavy-laden boughs.
A calming peace is summer's vow.
Now, cool, the air which ushers in,
as Autumn's changes now begin.
Leaves which turn to reds and gold;
days are short and nights are cold.
Harvest of each bounty fare.
Flowers die in brief despair.
Fallen leaves, upon the ground.
On the air, are echoed sounds.
Summer's loss, is Autumn's gain.
Each, in time, designed to change
more than landscape and the air -
thought and mood, which we declare.

Autumn

Margaret Taylor

The leaves flutter and fly all around
'til finally a carpet is laid on the ground.
All shapes and sizes; many colours too,
Gone to make way for everything new.
In the autumn season things slow down,
Before the Christmas rush comes to town.
Animals disappear into hibernation;
Birds fly away in yearly migration.
The farmers are busy out in the field,
Bringing in crops; they hope a good yield.
In churches many harvest queens are crowned.
An abundance of produce spread all around.
The witches arrive at this time of year,
Bringing with them dread and fear.
They weave magic spells, their own secret way
At Halloween on this October day.
November arrives with a sombre note,
As we think of the men who bravely fought:
Up in the air, on land and on sea.
We remember their sacrifice for you and for me.

Mold

Linda Ann Ford

There is something about Fall,
when the leaves are tumbling down,
when the wind begins to blow,
swirling them around...
They say it is the mold,
which grows upon the leaves.
But to me, I only know
I begin to cough and sneeze.
Some people are allergic
to dust and pollen spores.
But I have to be quite different
and look for something more.
So, when the leaves begin to turn
those rusty-colored hues...
Please excuse me for a time
while I just say, "ah-choo".

Fall

Rita Hodgson

All summer the slender Ginkgo
Danced behind fan shaped leaves.

Last week, yellowed with cold,
She glowed in the setting sun.

Now wind and rain have bared her limbs.
And paved my path with gold.

Reflections of Change

Joan M Crossley

He'd captured slow Autumn within her eyes,
Wind-whipped storms, dark-laden skies
Leaves green with life - now copper and red,
Turning brown and brittle like lumps of lead.

He knows the *last*...isn't that far ahead;
No welcoming fires, drawn shades or warm bed.
Time will move forward, but the clocks will go back;
Memories will linger - her love he'll not lack.
Whispers of change waft on rose-scented breeze,
Casting sweet shadows of life with ease.
Back to green earth she must somehow transport
Her sunshine and soul, so calmly sought.

Winter

Dining Out

Rita Hodgson

It's winter and the rain and wind
Keep folks indoors.
Spare a thought for the creatures
With no transport
And no central heating.

All autumn we have watched berries
Ripen and turn colour,
Black, purple, scarlet.
They are plump now and look
Luscious, ready to eat.

We have holly in our garden – I know it's a weed.
We have cotton easter (as we have always called it)
And, since we've been in Belgrave
We have the prolific ubiquitous Lilli pilli.

"My gran used to make lillipilli jam"
comments a friend.
Where is she now, when we need her?

In this bleak weather,
Small beaks dine on our weeds.

Rowan Trees

Mary J O'Rourke

"Jack, Jack. Come and look at this," called Jean from the front room. Jack appeared through the door leading from their small kitchen. Jean beckoned him over to the window.

"What's up love?" inquired Jack as he shuffled in his slippers over to the window.

"Look at that, it's a sight to behold," said Jean excitedly pointing in the direction of the three Rowan trees down the left side of their garden. "Now don't make a sound Jack or you will frighten them away, there must be a couple of hundred birds in the trees feasting on those berries".

The three Rowan trees in their communal garden were well-matured and quite large and Jean always marvelled at the beauty of them throughout the seasons. The white blossom in the Spring was absolutely gorgeous followed by the luscious looking bright red berries in the Summer and the early Autumn, and the best time of the year by far for Jean was the Autumn.

She loved it when all the small birds swooped down in unison to feast on the berries. Soon there would not be a berry in sight.

Hannah in the downstairs flat invited all the birds into the garden with the tit-bits she put out for her feathered friends: fat balls, nuts, bits of apple and bacon rind. Jack helped Hannah sometimes in the garden with the heavier jobs, but he wasn't as fit as he used to be. But between them it was well tended and tidy.

Jack toddled back into the kitchen to finish his chores muttering, he couldn't stay looking through the window all day like some folk did, alluding to Jean, jokingly of course.

Jack and Jean had been married almost 55 years and were getting on a bit themselves. You could say they too were in the Autumn years of their lives.

Jack suggested a walk down to the park after a bit of lunch because it was too nice a day to stay in and Jean agreed. "Righty-oh," said Jean. "Just give me a couple of minutes to get changed into something nice and put a bit of tutty on."

True to her word, a few minutes later she emerged from the bedroom looking very presentable. Jack smiled approvingly and winking at her said, "Let's go girl".

On their way down to the park they called in to their elder son's house with a birthday card and a voucher; they stayed just long enough for a cup of tea.

Jean remarked that it was on such a day as this that their son was born 47 years ago at 2:10 p.m. Jean has a fantastic memory, thought Jack, who rarely knew when his medical appointments were; he'd be lost without Jean…

The walk in the park was very pleasant, but after a couple of hours Jack was feeling tired and needed to go home: "You'll sleep tonight chuck," quipped Jean as she unlocked their front door and stepped inside. "Close the curtains dear, while I put the kettle on". After their cup of tea and a chicken sandwich, Jack fell fast asleep on the settee so Jean, who was feeling very contented, got out her latest library book, read for a while and went to bed looking forward to another day.

Creation's Secrets

Arthur Ives

Abby sidled up to me and said, "Papa."

"Yes, my sweet," I replied.

"Can we play with the duckies?" she asked.

Little Zara stopped searching her Mum's bag, and became alert for my reply.

"It's winter, love," I said regretfully. "It's wet and windy, and you've had colds.

Abby was four and Zara was two. Sometimes on pleasant days, we would plop the concrete mother duck and her three ducklings into the bird bath in the middle of our lawn. Time and I would stand still - but not so the girls. They would busy themselves, using their tiny hands as paddles, swirling the water this way and that around the island of ducks, collecting flowers, buds and leaves to float on the water's surface, wetting the sleeves of their tops, splashing me and each other, giggling at my discomfort and at the drenching they were giving themselves, lost in the bliss of play.

How many more days did I have left to enjoy life's simple pleasures? Sadly, too few.

Spring came on cue, and on the first warm day the girls visited, I was on duckie duty. The camellias were in bloom, and Abby discovered their soft pink petals could be removed to float with the other pickings. The petals of a single bloom were never ending. Even as she plucked off the last that had unfolded, there were more and more, bound tightly in the bud at the flower's centre, each, a smaller replica of the one before.

The little ones accepted miracles of nature as the way things were, but I, like a sentimental old fool, shook my head in wonder, and lamented the fact that I must soon be leaving, no wiser about creation's secrets than Abby and Zara were.

A Long Day for Eva

By Brian Croft

The year is 1913. It's six o'clock on a December morning and the snow has been heavy overnight. Young Eva has to struggle through the drifts on her way down from the farm on the wild Lancashire moors. A couple of miles walk down to the weaving mill on these dark winter mornings means chilblained feet and frosted up cheeks on the twelve-year-old's face. Her clogs and black stockings and her heavy shawl give her a little help in these northern winters but the deep snow clings to her feet and legs and by the time she reaches the warmth of the mill, she is shivering heavily and her black hair is wringing wet.

On days like this, she is happy to reach the warm noisy mill with its massive Lancashire Looms thundering around her, with the shuttles flying across; weaving sheets and cloths for the merchants in Manchester. Some of the older women work eight looms or more and they make sure that their young helpers like Eva are kept running about, clearing under the looms, helping with the beams of cotton and being at the beck and call of the Tacklers, who keep the looms working and supplied. These hard men ensure that all the people in their charge work like slaves, and the youngsters get many a clip around the ear for no apparent reason. The tacklers call it discipline! It is all very exhausting for the youngsters, especially when they have to put in a full day.

On two or three days during the week, Eva works in the mornings and then attends the local school. Basic reading and writing and sums are crammed in by a severe looking lady teacher, hair in a bun, and wearing a long skirt, who is always ready with a cane for any of the pupils who might display any sort of disobedience or laziness. Occasionally they will learn a little Geography or History and Eva really loves this. She reads of the faraway places and the knights of old and creates her own little dream world that takes her away from her hard northern life. There are not many books at school although the mill owner does sometimes buy a new set for the establishment, and these are grabbed by eager pupils. They are like gold dust and the children have to back them with brown paper to protect them before they are locked away in a big cupboard, in case any over eager child should want to show his or her parents how clever they are by taking them home to read. Many of their parents cannot read or write.

Eva's parents are quiet and caring; her father doesn't say much, but he rules the family in a strict but kindly way, whilst Mum is warm and loving and treats her children as her friends.

Out of school, Eva then has to go to the local shops to buy the food and supplies to take back to her parents and her three brothers on the farm. Much of the food that the family needs is produced by themselves. Eggs, milk, bread and butter are plentiful, and vegetables are grown out in the small field next to the cowshed, but she still needs to carry most of the other needs up the long steep moorland path.

Home at last, she can sit on the stool in front of the great fireplace and feel the lovely warmth and recite all her days' happenings to Mum and Dad and her brothers. Her best pal is her eldest brother John, who is always laughing and playing tricks. He can't wait to hear her tales of school and, because he had attended the same school before Eva, he knows all the teachers and has nicknames for them all, and has the family laughing at his impersonations. A big chubby lad who smiles all day, he had acquired an accordion some years ago, having swopped it for a dozen eggs. His mum was not pleased at first, but it gave the family such joy that she soon accepted it as the best bargain that family had ever made. He has taught himself to play some lively tunes, and most evenings, after the family have eaten their meal, he will fill the room with music whilst Eva dances around the heavy flagged floor, and the other lads clap and sing along with mum and dad. In the flickering firelight, these simple evenings are magical!

Before they can go off to their beds they have to check the animals outside and make sure that they are safe for the night. The fences, shippons and poultry sheds are looked over since intruders like foxes and rustlers are always a problem. Mum stays in and sorts the food and clothing for the family as well as turning the great barrel of a churn, producing fresh butter to supplement the family's tiny income. Eva sometimes has a go but it makes her arms ache and she wonders how her mum is so strong to be able to keep the barrel turning at such speed for so long.

Bedtime for Eva is earlier than the rest of the family and it is always preceded by Mum and her prayer. ....."Dear Lord, We thank you for today: We thank you for the food and drink: We thank you for our health and happiness and most of all we thank you for our wonderful family. Amen."

Eva knows that these winter days are hard but she is thankful for the warmth and love of her family and knows that she can look forward to the sunny days and happy times on the farm. Although it has been a long day she joins her mum in the prayer and smiles as she falls asleep. A Happy Girl.

A Winter's Tale

Nicola Ormerod

It was winter when you left and the snow clung to the ground coating everything in a blanket of white. Everything was serene and temporarily masked the uneasy atmosphere of the war. I was sixteen then and we had known each other for just under a year. I remember the day with perfect clarity...

I was buying some vegetables at the market. Food was scarce because of the war. You stood with your father selling a rabbit on another stall. I saw you and our eyes met briefly before I dropped my gaze coyly. Your hair was sandy blond and shone brightly in the morning sun. Your eyes were a piercing blue and your face, square and masculine for one so young.

As my gaze dropped, I saw the corners of your mouth turn up into a smile and you became even more handsome. That was the first time I'd ever seen you and yet after that day we ran into each other all the time. You asked me my name and I told you it was Edith, or Eidie as everyone called me. You told me your name was Charles.

An innocent courtship began; a different kind of courtship than today's youth knows. We held hands and took walks in the park. It was a month before we shared a kiss, and even that was just a small peck on my cheek.

I was aglow with love. You were handsome, the son of a farmer, strong and protective. And yet you gave me your jacket when there was a chill in the air and always held doors open for me. Always the perfect gentlemen.

We knew you would be enlisted to go to war and you were proud to serve your country and so two weeks before you were due to leave we made love, a bold reckless step on my behalf but I couldn't let you leave without sealing our love somehow.

We had a blissful few days where you snuck into our cottage after my parents had left for work. It was wonderful and we spoke of marrying as soon as you returned on leave. I gave you a picture of myself to take to show everyone your sweetheart back home.

I could have cried enough tears to melt the lingering snow after we saw you away on the train. My heart ached and ached and yet no one could understand why the parting was so bittersweet for me. I had tasted love and I ached for your touch once more.

Your father delivered the news two days into the New Year. You had died in combat. My photograph was tucked into your uniform pocket. Your father gave it me, complete with a bullet hole in the corner courtesy of the Jerries.

The pain in my chest was instantaneous and so sharp it took my breath away. I sagged to my knees and your father and my mother helped me to the couch. I sobbed and sobbed and your father, fresh with grief, sobbed too - we were united in our sorrow.

If coping with losing you wasn't enough, there came a further discovery. A part of you was growing within me.

My belly swelled with the babe growing in my stomach and I was both ashamed and overjoyed.

Ashamed for giving myself away before I had married and overjoyed your legacy would live on. I told your father first, breaking down. He was overjoyed, you'd been his only son but he understood my concern. He fetched my mother and father and they were upset but took it much better than I thought. Your father gave me your late mother's ring and from then on I took your surname and we told everyone that we'd married in secret the day you left for war.

The story was readily accepted and I was a widow without ever being married.

Spring approached and I had visited your father for eggs. He was planting out some trees on his land and had the small saplings all pulled up from the green house ready to plant and I had an idea.

When I told him he nodded, agreed that it was fitting and I went along and planted the trees with your father in the shape of a large heart on the hillside.

You couldn't see the shape really to start with, but just knowing it was there and the hard work that had been involved reassured me. As the time went on, I gave birth to your son, sandy hair and piercing blue eyes just like you. Your father retired to his sister's house and left me the farmhouse where our son, named Charles for his father and I, had many happy memories. With each passing year I would gaze out of the kitchen window and see my small wooded area growing on the hillside, a symbol of my love for you that never faltered or died.

As our son grew, he asked about you and I showed him pictures. I kept your memory alive even though I had so few memories myself. I loved my son. All the love I would have shown to you both was poured into him. He wanted for nothing and I feel I raised him well on my own. Before I knew it, he was a man, taking a mechanic's apprenticeship and courting a young lady. He finished his training and he got a house of his own, they married and began a family. He visited often, never forgetting about his old mum. I was so proud, as you would have been too.

One day just shortly after my seventieth birthday, Charles had visited; his wife was expecting their fourth child and I had begun knitting odds and sods, ignoring the arthritis than made my fingers stiff and awkward.

"Mum," Charles said casually sitting down. His eldest son, also named Charles for you, went to the toy box I kept near the fire and rummaged for a toy to entertain himself.

"Yes dear," I answered, putting down the baby hat I was working on.

"Why did you never remarry after dad died?"

I didn't need to hesitate with my answer it was simple and it always had been.

"I didn't even want to try and love anyone as much as I loved him."

As Charles stood and went to make himself tea and a sandwich I followed and gazed out to the hill; to the beautiful heart shaped wood on the side of the hill, thick and full and there for all to see and I know now as I knew then I would never find another you. I might have lost you before our love truly blossomed but a piece of you lives on in our son and grandchildren. Your legacy and bloodline never died and one day we will meet again.

Christmas is Cancelled

Peter Jones

Debbie checked her online account. It was December 23rd and her wage should have been in there yesterday. The page opened. It still wasn't there!

Frantically, Debbie searched her bag for her phone. She keyed in the company's number and got the switchboard.

"Hi, this is Debbie Fielding. Is there anyone in the office I can speak to please?"

"I'm sorry Miss Fielding, this is Simon on security. They've all left for the Christmas holidays."

"This is very important. Is there a number you can reach someone on. My wage hasn't been put into my bank account and I have presents to buy for my children."

"The only number I have is for the head of human resources, but he made it quite clear it was only to be used in emergencies."

Debbie was starting to feel herself getting a little angry and her voice hardly hid this with her next remark.

"What do you think this is? I have no money going into Christmas. I have eight people coming to join the four of us, but first I have to pick up the turkey and pay for it and buy all the food and drink besides. Bloody well ring him!"

With that, the line went dead and Debbie heard Abba. What seemed like an interminable five minutes went by and then a voice came on the line.

"Mrs Fielding. This is Harvey Reynolds from Human Resources. I believe you have an emergency?"

"Yes Mr Reynolds, I would call not being paid an emergency, wouldn't you?"

"I suppose I would, but there's very little I can do about it until January 2nd now. The whole system is in automatic lockdown until we return to work."

"What am I supposed to do at Christmas with no money? Can you tell me that? And why the hell didn't it go into my account?"

"I wish I had the answers you seek but I'm afraid I am as much in the dark as you. Is there no-one who could lend you some money and you can pay them back after Christmas?"

"Nobody I could bear to ask. None of my immediate family are that flush, and its Christmas for them as well." With that, Debbie slammed down the phone and started to cry.

Suddenly she had a thought. Her sister Imogen had once been in a similar situation and she had helped her at that time. Perhaps she would be in a position where she could return the favour – at least until after Christmas?

The dialling tone purred and after four rings, Imogen answered.

"His sis, Debbie here. I wondered if you could do me a big favour?"

"I will if I can Debs. What is it you want?"

Debbie proceeded to tell her sister the whole sorry tale. Imogen was suitably sympathetic and angry on her sister's behalf, but by the tone of her voice, Debbie knew there was a "but" on the way.

"That's awful Debs, but Darren was made redundant last month and there isn't a penny to spare at the moment. I really am sorry. You know I would do anything within my power to help if I could. Debbie desperately tried to hide her disappointment because she knew her sister was telling the truth.

"Oh God! What am I going to do now?" she said after putting down the phone.

There was only one thing for it. She would have to go online and borrow enough to tide her over from one of the Payday Loans companies. She hated them with a passion because of the way they advertised and their extortionate interest rates, but there was no other way. How could she let down her three kids, especially at this time of year? She burst into tears again at the thought.

Almost as soon as she stopped crying and regained her composure, there was a knock on the door.

Standing, hand poised for another round of knocking, as Debbie opened the door, was Angela, the wages clerk from work. Debbie was ready to give her a piece of her mind, but Angela held up her hands in mock surrender.

"Hi Debbie. I bet you noticed that you had no wage this month eh?"

"What do you think? What happened?"

"I'm afraid it's all my fault, there are two Deborah Greens on the payroll. You also have the same birthday. Only the year is different and I paid her both your wage and hers."

Debbie was getting a little agitated by this time.

"The other Deborah noticed it and rang in just before we left. She wanted your banking details so she could transfer the money, but of course we can't do that, so I went round to her house and transferred it on her behalf. The money should be in your account before the bank closes."

Debbie let out an audible sigh of relief.

"I thought I was going to have to tell the kids Christmas was cancelled this year."

Mags and Maggie

Stuart Hartley

Snow had been falling slowly all day and into the night. It descended like cotton wool orbs in slow motion. Everything seemed to be swathed in a glittering blanket of sparkling diamond dust. It danced in a kaleidoscope of reflected colours from the Christmas lights that draped the small tree in the library garden and from the large Christmas tree across the road. Seasonal lights twinkled merrily in windows and dancing lights on living room trees flashed merriment and brightness to those both inside and out. The streets lights glowed orange and gold everything conspired to deny the whiteness of snow.

As usually happens when everything is blanketed in billions of snowflakes, sound is muted and muffled. The quiet and stillness of night intensifies when snow lays thickly all around, covering everything with a cushioning mantle. All was as still and peaceful as one could hope for on a Christmas Eve. The distant muffled chiming of the Immanuel Church clock in New Lane was the only sound that penetrated the stillness as it struck the hour of one o'clock.

It was Christmas morning and all was well. Or at least all seemed to be well, except for the small shaggy and bedevilled dog that struggled through the deep snow as it plodded aimlessly down Havelock Street. He was weary and cold and was making slow progress to nowhere; except that he hoped it would be towards his home and a cosy warm fire. His tail hung down between his legs and his sagging ears intensified his miserable and dejected appearance.

Exhausted and fatigued he eventually crept into a doorway and immediately fell sound asleep.

Mrs Maggie Taggard listened to the church clock as it struck the hour. Once again, she went to her front door to shout for Mags. He had been missing for several hours, ever since he chased the cat from next door down the street. Chasing cats was one of his favourite activities, although he would never harm them, the chase was always fun and invigorating. Tonight, he must have become disorientated because of the snow, unable to sniff or find his way back home. At eleven years of age, it was not good for him to be out on such a cold frosty night and she was very worried about him.

Maggie occasionally slept throughout the day instead of at night. She had acquired this habit when her deceased husband Fred worked nights and she hadn't wanted to sleep on her own, so she adapted her routine to that of her husband's work — they had never slept apart. Her small living room was decorated in the traditional seasonal fashion; her sideboard and mantelpiece were covered with Christmas cards. Several small Christmas parcels were laid out on the hearth. She'd baked cakes, cooked a large turkey and ensured that there was a stock of vegetables, including beastly Brussel sprouts, ready for when her children and grandchildren came on Christmas Day.

Suddenly, there was a familiar scratching sound at the front door and Maggie knew immediately that Mags had found his way back home. She let him in and their joy at seeing each other was ecstatic. He shook off the snow that clung to his shaggy fur coat and ran to the fire, his tail wagging furiously, ears and eyes alert with an expression that said: 'Food - I'm hungry, what's to eat?'

During the rest of the early hours of Christmas morning, Mags and Maggie shared the turkey, the hearth and the fire, both loved and content in each other's company. It was a joyous night. Once again, all was well.

That Christmas, it became the gossip of Oswaldtwistle that old Mrs Taggard had been found dead in her armchair beside her fire on Christmas morning. There were signs that she had been celebrating Christmas when she had died. Later in the day, her dog Mags had been found dead, curled up in the local library doorway.

My Winters Remembered

Mary J O'Rourke

During the Second World War in the 1940s when I was
a little girl, I remember every winter that lots of snow fell
and stayed with us for what seemed like weeks and weeks.
It snowed whilst we were sleeping in our beds. Ever so
gently and softly it floated down, and when we woke up to
a beautiful white winter wonderland, we couldn't wait to
get outdoors. We slid and snowballed all the way to
school, it was magical.

As we sat in our classrooms, the snow continued to
come down, playtime and home time couldn't come soon
enough. All we could think of was going out to enjoy it.
We sledged down the slopes on Nelson Square on old
shovels, pieces of metal or wood; anything that could
accommodate a small bottom. We made glass like slippery
slides on our streets and in the playgrounds. They stayed
frozen for days and days, giving us so much pleasure.

We never wanted to go home; we were frozen to the
marrow and wet through with wellies full of melting snow
that made red rings of chapped skin where they flapped
against our little bare legs.

All the girls wore the regulation 'pixie-hoods' made out
of old scarves, sewn halfway down and with the ends
tucked across our bony chests.

We had great snowball fights against the Protestants
from the school up the lane, and we never wore gloves or
mittens and were always reluctant to go home, but when

155

we did we gulped our tea down to get out again to play under the street lamps. In the scrunchie snow, we built snowmen, huge snowmen. We never came to any harm or caused any damage, just innocent child-like fun.

As we went home to our beds; cold, wet, tired but happy, we couldn't wait for tomorrow to come to start all over again. Our house was cold and draughty, often without even a fire in the grate, only cold water to wash in and an outside long drop smelly lavatory where you froze to death whenever you went for a wee. We slept five to a bed top to toe to keep each other warm covered by old coats for blankets. But we accepted the good with the bad, because that is how a lot of families lived in those days. We survived.

Winter Soul

Gillian Jones

My mum loved roses. The front garden of our family home was abundant with rose bushes; different varieties, all shades of colour, some in full flower, and the rosebuds about to disclose their exquisite secrets. Throughout the summer months when they were in bloom, walking up the garden path was a calming and uplifting experience, the senses assaulted with the sight and fragrance of the blooms. I declare that only the most hardened heart wouldn't have been captivated by its beauty.

In the far corner of the garden, there was a rose bush that had refused to flower for a number of years. Each year it produced an abundance of dark green leaves, but it didn't produce one rose. One year my dad said to mum that if the rose bush didn't flower this particular year, he was going to dig it out. This surprised the family, as dad had never shown an interest in the garden. It was mum that always tended to it, but she told him 'no' and to give it another year or so, as apart from no roses appearing, it was healthy looking rosebush.

Summer passed, autumn arrived and then winter followed. In early January, the start of another new year, the year that it was possible that the defiant rose bush that wouldn't flower could be no more if dad had his way, tragedy struck.

Our gentle, quietly spoken dad died suddenly, a few days into that New Year. He hadn't complained of feeling unwell when he retired to bed, but the following morning as he and the rest of the family wakened to another day, he collapsed and died. He was only sixty-two.

Grief, bereavement, is a bruising life event to deal with. Whether the death of a loved one is anticipated or it's sudden, the pain is all-encompassing. To say the family were in shock at dad's passing so suddenly was an understatement.

The day of the funeral arrived all too quickly and it was a time when wreaths were delivered direct to the house. It was a bright, crisp, bitterly cold January day with a dusting of snow covering all that you could see. It took me back to another winter's day a few years before, a day that was so special to me, because on that day my dad and I shared one of those special father and daughter moments. It was November and I was getting married. The day before the wedding was a miserable winter's day; it was damp, cold, and the sky was overcast. I had the wedding jitters and the gloomy day made them worse. I was convinced that the wedding day would be as gloomy as the weather. Dad, a man of few words who only spoke when he thought it was necessary, told me not to get upset or worry as the weather would be perfect for my wedding day.

The morning of my wedding, before anyone else awoke from their slumber, and the dawn had just broken through, my lovely dad brought me a cup of tea. He instinctively knew that I would have slept very little. He told me to drink my cuppa, not to look out of the window, and then to come downstairs, which I duly did. Dad took my hand, smiled and then opened the front door. Greeting us was the bluest of skies and a beautiful winter sun. A dusting of snow had fallen overnight and the sun made it look as though millions of diamonds had fallen on the snow. It made the landscape look magical. There was a hushed silence; peacefulness. I knew then that all was as it should be.

But back to this awful day as the wreaths were lying along the garden path, I could stand it no more and decided I needed to go for a walk to get away, if only for a short while, from the palpable grief that hung in the house. I was bereft at the sudden loss of my dad and I was very angry that he had been denied the opportunity to enjoy retirement which he was so looking forward to, or to see my three younger siblings fly the nest and go out into the world. Nor would he see my two toddler sons grow; they adored their granddad, but most of all I was angry that he had left me and I hadn't had the chance to say goodbye. I wasn't there with him when he died. As I walked out of the front door to go for a walk with this rage and anger bottled up inside of me, through my tears my gaze was drawn to the far corner of the garden; to that stubborn rose bush that had refused to flower for all those years.

I had to wipe away my tears to make sure I wasn't imagining what I saw, because, even though it was a bitter cold January day with snow on the ground, there on that defiant rose bush, was the most complete rosebud, enclosed in three perfect dark green leaves. In that instant I knew that dad was telling me that he would always be with us, the family. It gave me enormous comfort and strength. I have never analysed what I saw; to me it's one of those experiences that doesn't need an explanation - it happened. Life is like that. At times, something happens to us that offers no explanation, no rhyme or reason.

Many, many years have passed since that day. I still miss my dad but there is no sadness. I know he's always with me because he's in my heart. And on those perfect, crisp winter days that happen, when the sky is so blue, the wintry sun is shining through and making the snow sparkle like diamonds, that's when I feel dad's presence even more, that's when I'm closest to him and I'm at peace with the world. My dad is my Winter Soul.

Otto's Winter Heist

Charlotte Youds

Quite late one night, I tell you true,
I came downstairs to make a brew,
And to my surprise I came upon,
Big Otto, the neighbour's thieving tom.

His head was shoved into my own cat's food,
And Otto was in a petulant mood,
For when I shouted 'bugger off!',
He glanced at me, yet still he scoffed.

His back arched up and as I came closer,
He licked and lapped at the empty saucer,
Hoovering up every morsel and bite,
Then shooting past like a rocket in flight.

Otto zoomed on by, his big black frame,
Dodging me without hint of shame,
And having successfully scoffed his prize,
He squeezed out through the cat flap half his size.

It was then that I noticed the snow falling down,
Big flakes settling on the pure white ground.
There in the middle of the thick drifting snow,
Sat Otto the felon, licking his paw.

I gingerly stepped out into the night,

Four Seasons

The cold was so sharp that I felt it bite.
Otto spotted me and got ready to flee,
But as I looked at him, he stared back at me.

I knew then he'd been locked out of his home,
No sensible cat would willingly roam,
In the freezing December air outside,
Where there's nothing to do but shelter and hide.

In silence we exchanged a knowing look,
And my heart did melt for the sneaky crook,
His big green eyes watched me carefully now,
As he let out the most pitiful meow.

I had to forgive the cat his misdeed
He was cold and wet and needed a feed,
Poor Otto had nowhere warm to go,
To flee the ice and the gathering snow.

But then he stood and turned his back.
To my dismay, his ears went flat.
He hunched his back, his tail went up,
He squatted, showing me his rump.

I hopped and shouted from where I stood:
Ranted and cursed, but it did no good,
The snow and my slippers had me stuck,
As Otto the scoundrel dropped his muck.

His work done, he slyly made his escape.

Jumped onto the wall as I watched agape,
And though I was filled with ire and sorrow,
I know he'll be back for more tomorrow.

Sometimes

Dorothy Clarke

Childhood Sweethearts 1947,
And sometimes when we stood there
With the winter winds blowing wild,
With cruel gusts, across the playground,
Then, he held his hand in mine.

Drinking ice-cold milk through plastic straws,
Sitting together by the roaring stove;
This gentle child would whisper true:
My friendship, always, is here with you.

And sometimes in the daffodil spring,
When we were nine, in spring time ring,
We gathered bluebells beside the stream,
Where all the trout rose in a silver gleam.

In the wild flower meadow where we played
And his father, the farmer, made the hay.
Summer's day, so happily spent;
Carefree hours, yet only lent.

Autumn danced now on the bramble ledge,
And a red robin chirped on the thicket hedge.
And we caught the leaves as they tumbled down
And picked ripe blackberries, autumn's crown.

Two Continents

The little village, covered in snow;
Trees sparkling white, moon hanging low.
Children skating hand in hand.
Our childhood days, spent in Wonderland.

Seasoned Greetings from Oz

Rita Hodgson

Immigrants have brought traditions with them.
Our imported festivals make more sense
North of the equator.

They celebrate the birth of the Christ Child
And the New Year
After the winter solstice,
When the sun finally starts to show itself
Earlier each day.

Here, the days are shortening.

They observe Lent, that frugal season.
When food is scarce, and they await
The earth's next bounty.

Here, we are in the middle of harvest.

They welcome Easter, with eggs, lilies and rabbits,
When sprouting seeds haze the earth with green
And the air is heavy with the promise of new life.
Here, it is the last long weekend before winter,
– An ideal time to finish painting the house.

After harvest in the misty autumn they have
Halloween, and Thanksgiving,

Two Continents
Inappropriately timed here,
In the spring racing carnival

So we have extra blessings.
All things happen twice,
Once, traditionally, with the rest of the world,
(which we season with a pinch of salt)
And again when the year dictates,
(which we relish alone)

But what, oh what do we do on our Vernal Equinox?
Theirs contains the promise of Passover and Easter.
While on ours, we worm the dog,
And check the smoke-alarm batteries.
It's worth more than that!

Each year, in September, on our twelve hour day,
Let us hold a special festival, to celebrate
The coming of spring to this blessed land of Oz,
While the rest of the world looks on,
Amazed at our good fortune.
A party is being arranged!

Winter, What Winter

David Berry

If you think your winters are cold, dream on.

Hi, my name is Kaaliya, (that means a huge serpent). We live in North Alaska in the Arctic.

I live with my mum and dad, brother and sister, and my grandparents. Dad doesn't have an Eskimo name. He's called Scott! He's 42 years old; how weird is that: Granddad called him that after the explorer Walter Scott. Scott went to the Antarctic and sadly died with his friends. Don't get me wrong, I have a lot of admiration for people like Scott - adventurers - but you would never find Eskimos sleeping in a canvas tent at minus 40°C, no way.

We live in igloos, eco-friendly homes built from snow. They are both environmentally and financially friendly. They cost us nothing but time to build and the material is free and plentiful. We are just about to build new ones for our winter camp. We always move closer to Ankara for winter to get supplies of whale blubber from the whaling fleet.

Anyway, here's the rest of my family. I've told you about Dad; now for Mum. Mum is 39 years old. Her name is Teresa. 'What?' I hear you say. Well her name came from Mother Teresa, a religious Indian lady, who dedicated her life to care for the poor. Grandpa saw her once on something called a television and was so inspired by her work, and called Mum after her. In our world, you have to all work together to survive. Mum is OUR Mother Teresa.

Then there's my sister Kaalika, (her name means blackness). Well she does have very black hair I suppose. She's 17, ambitious, beautiful and focused. My brother, Bjorg, who is fifteen (yes you've guessed it), is named after Bjorn Borg the tennis player. I call him Fifteen-love – he calls me Sid, after Sid the Snake.

Gran and Grandpa are amazing. Gran Kirma - that means hill. Strange eh? We don't have that many hills here in our northern desert - yes desert. Do you know which is the largest desert in the world? No? The Antarctic.

It's not about sun and sand, it's how much recorded rainfall you have in a year. We don't get much rain here in the Arctic. Gran has a polar bear skin Grandpa got for her 40th birthday years ago. She sleeps under it.

Then there's my beloved Grandpa Yoskolo (that means to break sugar pine cones). There ain't many pine trees here either. He's such an inspiration to all of us. He is our survival. What he doesn't know about the harsh world we live in, you could write on a full stop. He's knowledgeable, patient, and cares a lot.

Dad and Bjorg have started our two igloos; they cut blocks of snow and obviously cross the joints like building a wall to make them strong. Each joint is packed with snow to seal them and keep out the blizzards and icy wind. They're surprisingly warm and we all feel safe in them.

It's hard work for both of them to form the roof part. Dad goes inside the part-built igloo, and as the roof is the trickiest bit, Dad leans forward against the snow blocks like a template, and his arched stance makes a perfect support for each block. It's a simple form of physics really. Force against force. Equal mass, against equal mass, against centrifugal force. We may be nomads, but we do have brains you know.

Suddenly, they've finished one igloo. Just the entrance and smoke hole left to make.

Grandpa says we should go and catch fish for tea. Like I said before, he is an expert. We are camped above a frozen lake and sea trout and what you call wild Alaska salmon are on our menus. Gran, Mum and Kaalika all work on the skins we hunted in summer to make new footwear and warm clothes for us.

Grandpa cuts a hole in the ice then listens. He uses entrails in the water to attract the fish. You might wonder, how does he know when a fish is attracted by this decomposing gunge? But he listens with his ear to the ice, smiles and says, "This is a good place. They will come here soon. Maybe a seal." That would be brilliant. He lowers a hook and line in the water and very quickly there is a sharp tug on the lines. Grandpa snatches the line back. Soon he lands a good-sized trout One strike and the thrashing stops. Tea's caught.

Grandpa says, "More near," so the line is back in our fishing hole. Three more fish caught. He's such a genius my Grandpa. Then the pièce de résistance: a plump arctic seal. How has he learnt these skills? Food, candles to make, skin for shoes. Nothing will be wasted with this catch. I get the job of dragging the seal back to camp. In case a polar bear gets the scent; they're fearsome predators, we would have no chance against these powerful animals. We do hunt and kill them, but not today.

We bury the seal in the frozen ground for safety, some distance from our igloos. Grandpa tells me we will mark our area North, South, East and West of the food store - basically a square around the area so we can find it later to skin and butcher it - again not at the camp. Polar bears can smell seal more than two miles away.

Back at camp, both igloos have been built: sealed and safe homes for all of us. There isn't much privacy for any of us, but that's our lives and we can retire to one of the other igloos if any of us need quality time on our own.

Mum and Kaalika (who's in a dark mood, get it, Kaalika means blackness) prepare and cook the trout. Everyone is happy about the seal. Hard to chew, but tasty. We'll go back tomorrow to butcher it. Dad and Grandpa reminisce about past hunts and the big ones soon to be. Bjorg, me and Dad this time. Grandpa deserves to relax more and try to retire. Our first night in our new homes. It's cosy and safe.

Overnight, one of our many blizzards has hit us, so basically we have to dig out our igloo. How are me and Grandpa going to find our seal? He seems to have some sort of built in gyroscope, so off we go and 15 minutes later, we dig it up, skin it and butcher it. Loads of seal meat. We don't need a freezer. It'll keep.

Grandpa, always cautious, looks for any sign of polar bear activity: tracks, tail trails, yellow urine marks. Clever stuff. I love my Grandpa.

If he says it's safe, it is, so we start to make tracks to the camp. Grandpa talks excitedly about his trip with Dad to Ankara for the whale blubber. Eskimo whale hunters only kill for our people to survive. We are all very conscious of our environmental responsibilities. We don't have supermarkets and we only take from our desolate environment what we actually need, no more, no less.

Soon we're back. Everyone is so excited about the seal, a very big catch for us. Grandma has been teaching Kaalika Eskimo skills with skins and Kaalikia is excited to show us what she has made for Bjorg and me. Eskimo designer gear. I give her a hug. She's a lovely sister.

Dad has promised to take Kaalika to Ankara when he goes with Grandpa in three more sleeps. I'll miss them all. It will be her first time going so I hope she'll like it.

Well Dad knows where to find driftwood for our fire on the shore of our frozen lakes, so it's off to get some. Everyone else is dealing with the seal's storage. We don't have much. No electric or gas gadgets, but each day is an exciting challenge here. I'm lucky I have everything a fourteen-year-old boy needs. My lovely grandparents, flexible Mum and Dad, pain in the butt brother, and lovely sister. I'm lucky and happy. Are you?

Winter

Margaret Taylor

The branches on the trees are drab and brown;
No smiles on faces. Only a frown.
The people around all feeling quite sad,
Well winter's begun; how can we be glad?
We awake in the morning; what is that glow?
The trees are amazing, all covered in snow,
Our dreams have come true, everything's grand,
In this fantastic, winter wonderland.
Children on sledges speeding down hills,
Screaming, excited at spills and thrills.
Snowmen are built in all different poses:
Buttons for eyes and carrots for noses.
Christmas shopping now in full swing,
All around you can hear the bells ring.
Children with lanterns sing Silent Night,
All the gifts bought, everything just right.
Christmas at last is almost here:
Our most favourite time of the year,
With trimmings all round and presents galore,
We are happy at last. Who could want more?

Four Seasons

Snowflakes

Rita Hodgson

The cold wind gusts through humid air.
Motes of vapour, chilled beyond bearing.
Clasp each others' hands,
Change state, chill out,
And start a stately dance.

Watch as they fall,
Each snowflake unique,
Each dance different

All together? – altogether perfect.

The Peaceful Garden

Joan M Crossley

The garden shimmered in the early morning sunshine. Green lawns and hedges had turned white with frost overnight.

"Good morning Robert Robin, bit nippy today," warbled Bertie Blackbird, cocking his gleaming black head, whilst searching the lawn for a tasty worm.

His orange beak began knocking against very hard ground. Bertie's dark eyes were surrounded by yellow circles, so eager to spot something to eat, but there were no worms, insects or fresh berries to be seen. Robert Robin, was perched on the highest branch of an old oak tree.

"Good day Bertie. Yes, I must say old chap, it's rather chilly this morning. If I were you, I'd fly up here and wait for Mrs Campbell to come out with her tasty treats," stated Robert, puffing up his bright red breast, and beginning to preen under his tiny wings.

But Bertie flew towards the pond, and landed on a rock. "At least the pond's not frozen," he sang happily, taking a drink of cool water, before joining his friend on a frosty branch.

"How are the family doing Robert? Bertie asked, shaking his black feathers. "It's a while since they flew the nest".

"Oh, they've spread their wings all right, they went last spring," Robert warbled sweetly. "Jenny, Ronnie, and

175

Roger have all flown off to bird college, but Mrs Roberta Robin is feeling lonely now. Perhaps we'll have more chicks to feed this coming spring or summer," he added with a sad hopeful warble. "We hope so anyway."

There was silence in the peaceful garden....

Suddenly, the feathered friends heard Mrs Campbell's kitchen door opening.

"Here we go Robert! It looks like Mrs Campbell has got some meal worms for you."

Kind Mrs Campbell stumbled over her grandson's old rusty bicycle and almost slipped on the icy path, as she carried some fat-balls and tiny pieces of fruit and crumbly cake and cheese to the bird table.

"Silly that! Mrs Campbell should've got rid of that bike years ago. After all her grandson Simon is into computers, X-box and mobile phones these days," cheeped Robert Robin.

Bertie Blackbird shook his orange beak saying, "She shouldn't be wearing her slippers. We'd better hurry up or the blue -tits and sparrows will eat everything!"

Mrs Campbell was closely followed by Jack her small terrier. "Woof- woof!" he barked, his tail wagging furiously as he sniffed, then followed the scent of the cake...

Robert Robin cheeped, "Huggh! You wouldn't think all dogs are supposed to be descended from wolves would you? Jack doesn't howl like one. No. He just yaps all the time, not much of a voice eh Bertie?"

The neighbour's door opened, and out rushed Cathy Cat, followed by two small children, dressed in their pyjamas, and their mother shouting, "Molly! James! Come in and get dressed. It's freezing out there..."

What a rumpus! The tousled haired children were running around wildly in their own garden, whilst Jack began barking persistently, at the dividing fence. "Woof-woof!"

Cathy jumped on the fence, hissing, and the children's mother tried to calm the cat, whilst trying to get Molly and James back indoors.

About twenty birds now perched in the high trees and hedges, just waiting to get their breakfast. They began singing, whistling, chattering or chirping loudly and impatiently.

"So sorry about all the noise, this morning," called Mrs Campbell across the frosty fence. "I'll take Molly and James for a walk to the park with Jack afterwards."

On hearing the word walk, Jack immediately pricked up his ears and sat down on the frozen lawn wagging his tail.

"Oh plea----ease mummy?"

Molly and James yelled, "Oh thank you! Mrs Campbell I can feed baby Edward in peace. I can hear him crying now. But I need to give Molly and James their breakfast first, they must be hungry as those birds by now. They've been running around all morning. They're so disappointed they can't take their small bicycles out in the garden, but it's so slippery out here isn't it?" replied Beth, the children's mother.

"Can we have ice-cream for breakfast?" asked Molly and James piped up,

"Oh can we mum?"

"No. Certainly not. Don't be silly, it's far too cold. I'll make you a lovely boiled egg each, with toasted soldiers. Much better to set you up for your walk with Mrs Campbell and Jack!" replied Beth with a shake of her head, "Come on in! You two need to get washed and dressed first. I'm switching that TV off. Exercise and a good walk in the crispy fresh air will do you more good."…

When the birds had finished enjoying their tasty morsels, the garden became peaceful and silent once more.

A short while later, Mrs Campbell set off with Jack the terrier and two small, warmly dressed children. They would enjoy a walk to the local park, and perhaps the children would feed the ducks with food that Mrs Campbell carried in her shopping bag. Then they could play on the cold roundabout and swings and have lots of fun…

Meanwhile, back in the garden. It was so peaceful again…

White snowflakes began to fall gently, and Robert Robin and Bertie Blackbird settled down to quiet conversation discussing the daily newspapers and the world at large. They both wondered when on earth spring and summer would finally arrive…

Winter

Linda Ann Ford

I am the crystal icicles,
hanging from your rooftops
like forgotten Christmas decorations.
I am a landscape
transformed by the heavy snows of winter
and the brushing winds of chance.
I am the etchings of nature,
playing upon your frosted window glass.
I am the colored flocks of birds,
busily feeding at the feeders.
I am the hardship of wildlife,
struggling through the deepening snows,
foraging for food.
I am the playground of the skier,
the snowmobiler, the skater and the sledder.
I am the rest for plant life,
and the watering of the earth.
In me there is cold, dark and gray - yet,
in me, there is rest, warmth and comfort.
None are so alive,
as those who survive through the harshness of my days...
and the promise that I always keep -
to give way to Spring.

The Summer Storm at Christmas

Margaret Gregory

The thunder cracked overhead, so close to the flash of lightning that it might have been simultaneous.

At the same moment, the lights went out, the air conditioning went off, and worst of all – the electric oven.

"Damn! The turkey is only half cooked, and the vegetables still have to go in. How are we to have Christmas dinner ready? Our guests will be here in an hour."

"Maybe 'they' will get the power back on soon," the young husband said, trying to calm his frantic wife.

It was as if the thunder had rattled the celestial icebox open. A barrage of hail and rain battered against the west facing windows.

"That is if our guests will be able to get here at all," the young husband commented.

"Come and see the front lawn. It looks like it has been snowing. That cool change certainly came with a vengeance."

"Yeah," the young wife agreed with a faint laugh.

"Trust Melbourne weather!"

Elsewhere, not too far away, the conversation was different.

When the power went off, another young wife was eyeing her husband, and seeming to be waiting for something.

"At least everything is ready. The cold meats and salads will keep well enough in the fridge," her mother assured everyone.

"And no one has to travel in this mess to get here. We can get the candles out to see to eat."

The sharp beeps of the pager cut through the chatter of the group that were family and friends.

"Warrick, your pager went off," his brother-in-law loudly stated the obvious. But Warrick was already using the phone to call up the electricity supply control centre, and had grabbed the nearest pen and paper to scribble down details by torch light. Then he ended that call and dialled another number.

"We're wanted," Warrick said into the phone.

"A feeder has dropped out, and we have a report of a tree down in Station Street, as well as a dozen other reports of no power."

Warrick, the on-call emergency linesman, grabbed his overalls, and his wet weather gear, kissed his wife and said, "Save some dinner for me. If I am lucky, I might get it for breakfast."

"Take care," his wife told him.

"Maybe next Christmas will be our first together."

"Don't get wet," his brother-in-law chuckled.

Warrick, one of the mysterious 'they', went out into the windy, icy, slippery, wet weather to fix the power.

Two hours later, the power came back on, and a chorus of, "Thank you, God," went silently up to heaven.

Another three hours later, God's soggy helper walked back in the door just as the clock struck midnight.

Winter's on the Way

Barbara Scott

Old Bob sat in the sun, enjoying the gentle warmth creeping into his bones. He determined to make the most of it, knowing that winter was not far off. He could see it in the garden; the trees were losing their lively green covering, some of them exchanging it for autumn glory, which announces for them a time of rest. He could sense the change too, in the sound of their branches creaking when they swayed in the breeze - that was cooler lately. Just like me, he thought as he moved his legs in order to stand.

'I wonder if the trees feel the same aching in their limbs?' Bob wondered.

'Well, I guess it is this time of life, for me and the trees; they must have their rest and wake in the Spring to produce more life. And it's not so bad. I have earned my retirement and been rewarded with memories – and a sort of humble satisfaction with the life I have led, and what I leave behind'

'I think that the best I leave behind is my family, my children and grandchildren; some great-grandchildren now. That must be my "immortality", I like to think of it that way. They will live on, perhaps creating more life. Some might produce things of beauty or discover more about this world and make life better for others... Well, enough of this maudlin, the fun's not over yet, I'll get on to Jack. Meet him down town and we can "chew the fat"'.

Bob fished his mobile out of his pocket and dialled the number.

'What's the matter with old Jack? - He's taking his time to answer. Probably fiddling on that danged invention of his and can't hear the phone. Needs a hearing aid, I reckon'.

Just as Bob closed the phone, a cloud came across the sun and left him in the shadow. He sat down once more to ease the aching bones, and closed his eyes. Where were all those positive thoughts he had been turning over in his mind? It was cold now. He pulled his coat over his shoulders and nodded off.

"Was I dreaming? That was Jennifer, I'm sure; calling out to me. But it couldn't be. She's been gone for years; although it only seems the other day when we would walk around the garden, my arm around her. So comfortable. Mmmm. And who is that with her? Ah! Little Esther. Our eldest child. We had her with us for a good fifty years, I reckon. A great fifty years. How lovely to see them again. I think I'll stay asleep for a little longer. To hell with that dinner gong, forget it. This dreaming is better. "

Zodiac.

Rita Hodgson

When I wish to view eternity
I do not go to visit man-made towers.
For me the sight of waters slipping by
Tall trees on the river bank is enough.
The re-assurance that the past and future
Meet in the present,
In the here and now.

When I wish to view eternity
I sit and gaze up at the night sky,
Wait for the wind to tidy up the clouds,
Wiping the tears from the eyes of the stars.

Then using the earth as my viewing platform,
The centre of my universe, where my feet are planted,
I can see clusters of points of light.

And I wonder at the time that has passed
Since man first gave the Zodiac names,
And used the moon and stars to mark the year.

The idea of eternity is too big
For my human brain to grasp.
Both time and space, which have no boundaries,
Live in my mind, firmly enclosed in my own experience.
That way lies sanity.

Four Seasons

Yct I am aware that eternity exists,
And that it is encompassed,
Neither by natural wonders,
Nor by man made towers.
What a Wonderment!

186

Made in the USA
Charleston, SC
28 May 2014